Presentations that Ignite Your Audience
More WOW. More Quickly.

by
Emma Sutton

First published in 2015 by:

The Solopreneur Publishing Company Ltd.
West Yorkshire WF9 4PU
www.thesolopreneur.co.uk

The publisher makes no representation, expressed or implied,
with regards to the accuracy of the information contained in this
book, and cannot accept any responsibility or liability.

ISBN 978-0-9931880-1-5

Printed in the U.K. by Charlesworth Press, Flanshaw Lane,
Wakefield WF2 9LP

ABOUT THE AUTHOR
Emma Sutton – Queen of Diamonds

After her initial nerves at speaking and presenting (yes, her mouth was dry), she rapidly developed an innovative approach that had people entranced from her opening line to her closing call to action. With her experience delivering presentations and workshops in the private, public and charitable sectors, throughout the UK, as well as in Europe and USA, she has a wealth of experience on which to draw.

Since leaving her scientific career, she has focused on delivering presentations and workshops on themes as diverse as Cancer Awareness, Creativity, Chemistry and Communication. She has coached organisations such as the NHS, Cancer Research UK and Birmingham University to deliver powerful presentations using her unique SPARK process and coached individuals such as Judy Parsons (author of Link Up with LinkedIn) and Tess Hornsby-Smith of Leeds University to find the Diamond within their topic and presentations.

As a Member of the Professional Speaking Association and an Award-Winning Speaker*, Emma is passionate about helping individuals and businesses to share their expertise and their passion with others through presenting and speaking, whilst helping ensure that what they say is Unforgettable. She also trains businesses to get a WOW when they answer the question "what do you do?" She regularly speaks to business networking groups, professional networks, and more. This enables individuals and businesses to stand out and shine, even in a crowded marketplace.

(*voted Speaker of the Year by the Professional Speaking Association in Scotland)

Contact information for Emma –

If you're struggling to focus and can't find your Diamond for the fluff, discover your sparkle with Emma Sutton, the Queen of Diamonds www.nakedpresenting.co.uk.

Keep Your Inspiration Stoked
For extra information, articles, videos and more on the theme of Presentations That Ignite Your Audience, go to Emma's website page dedicated to helping your Presentations Ignite Your Audience and have more WOW at www.nakedpresenting.co.uk/ignite

Twitter is:
http://www.twitter.com/nakedpresenting
Facebook is:
https://www.facebook.com/DiamondPresenting
LinkedIn is:
http://www.uk.linkedin.com/in/emmasutton

ABOUT THE 'SOLOPRENEUR'S GUIDE' SERIES

This book - indeed, every book in the 'Solopreneur's Guide' series - is different from most other business guides or titles. It's not structured chapter by chapter; instead, the content is laid out in such a way that it answers solopreneurs' most frequently asked questions on a given topic or discipline.

So, what is a 'solopreneur'?

The term 'solopreneur' is used when talking about 'Independent Professionals' (or 'IPs'). There are many similarities between solopreneurs and entrepreneurs; in the context of our books and series, by describing a business owner as a solopreneur, we're referring to people who are completely reliant on their own personal brand in order to make a living (essentially, 'one-person-brands').

What else is unique about the 'Solopreneur's Guide' series?

When researching the merit of business books, feedback showed that solopreneurs found many titles hard to relate to – particularly those written by successful, or well-known, business leaders. Though solopreneurs felt some information within these books was valuable, they said the 'golden nuggets' were hidden from masses of pretentious, technical, or irrelevant text. They were also disappointed that the majority of business books failed to offer direction on how to apply the authors' advice within the average solopreneur business. As a result, the business owners we spoke to felt that many authors of non-fiction 'business books' didn't understand them or their needs.

Most businesses – even global corporations – have to start somewhere. Having a small business does not mean the owner has little ambition, nor is it a measure of how successful the business will remain as time advances. The right kind of information, applied at the right time, will help more businesses grow – which is where this series comes in. We've sourced the best experts in each field: qualified and experienced professionals - whose target markets are made up of solopreneurs and small business owners – who will impart useful, appropriate information, in an easy-to-apply format.

In today's society, people want to fast-track their understanding of a subject and any subsequent results. The advent of the Internet has made knowledge more accessible than ever, but nothing can replace the added ingredient of experience within that framework.

The authors chosen to write for the 'Solopreneur's Guide' series are already recognised experts with a credible track record. They understand their customers – and, in turn, their readers - and the problems they commonly face.

These experts are accessible, which we feel is important, should you like more information or tailored advice. They're not unattainable or out of reach – all 'Solopreneur's Guide' authors are business owners, just like you. Contact information will be included in all books, relating to the author in question, as well as links to any free downloads/resources/training in the ABOUT THE AUTHOR section, at the beginning of each book.

Every 'Solopreneur's Guide' author is active on social media and welcomes your feedback.

CONTENTS

Introduction

INTRODUCTION

Whatever your business, there is no doubt that you need the skills to talk to groups of people and have them pay attention and listen to you. You need to be able to influence others, to lead them, to  convince them to buy from you or to share your vision for your company's future.

Yet many people are afraid of presenting. They purposely avoid situations where they might be the centre of attention or have to talk to a group. As a powerful way to market your small business, (I have personally converted strangers to clients in just a five-minute presentation), you cannot afford to deliver a presentation that does not Ignite Your Audience.

And not all presenters are good at it. The fact that you can stand at the front of the room and talk does not confer the status of a "good presenter" on you. You need to be able to do far more than just talk to a group of people to Ignite Your Audience.

This book is for you if:
- You want your presentation and your business to stand out in a crowded room
- You want your presentation to inspire new ideas and passion in your audience

- You want your presentations and your business to be remembered
- You want your audience to be hanging on your every word
- You want to do all this in a fraction* of the time you usually take

Just one step in this book helped Sarah Fox of 500words to cut the preparation time for her construction law courses from one week to just one day!

A Presentation that Ignites Your Audience

Whether you want to inspire potential clients with the promise of your new product, or tell a roomful of strangers in sixty seconds about your business, you have an amazing opportunity before you.

You have an opportunity to create an experience using the power of your words. Chosen well, you words will uplift, inspire, engage, excite and change the lives of the people in your audience. Your presentation can ignite new ideas, new attitudes, and new skills in just a few minutes. It can encourage your audience to do things they have never done before.

It was a presentation that gave me the confidence to do something I thought was impossible, or at least highly unlikely. One charismatic person delivered words that persuaded me to walk over red-hot coals. With no fear. Feeling 100% confident that I could do it. It was at that moment that I knew I wanted too wanted to become a presenter.

So what could you do? What difference could you make, if only you had the perfect words coupled with powerful resources to help your message ignite your audience?

Whether you want to inspire them into sharing your vision for your company or ignite them into action, you cannot afford to deliver words that are confusing or boring.

For you to make the most of the amazing opportunity you have in front of you, you need to create a presentation with SPARK!

Presentations Are Powerful
As a way of spreading the message about yourself or your organisation, presentations are the ultimate marketing tool. You can speak once and have hundreds of people listen to you at a live event, with the potential to reach many thousands more through posting the recording online.

By speaking to groups, you will:
• Establish yourself as the expert in your field. This book happened because Gail at Solopreneur heard me speak on presentation skills.

- Demonstrate your own abilities and skills. It gives people a chance to "try before they buy" so they know that they are going to get great value in working with you.
- Fast-track the know-like-trust sequence. Clients who heard me speak for just five minutes have then hired me, despite the fact they were strangers at the start.
- You can reach far more people, worldwide, with a single presentation. One presentation I delivered online reached 600 people from India to the USA.

One Presentation One Hundred Products
This book is written for those of you who are going to present – that is to speak live to an audience of people. Your audience might be small or huge, your time might be short or long, your venue might be your local church or a huge stadium.

However, the process you use to develop this material can help you create hundreds of products or services, such as:
- On-line Webinars delivered live, or recorded and then given away or sold
- E-books or printed books. This book started as a one-day workshop
- Teleseminars delivered in the audio version only
- Workshops and seminars where you develop your presentation into an interactive "how to" process with live coaching and feedback
- Blogs and articles for online or offline printing

and reading

The time you invest in learning to be a great presenter will pay for itself handsomely. There is hardly a day when I am not presenting myself, my ideas or information to individuals or groups of people.

The skills you will learn from following the answers to these five questions will help you to talk more confidently and eloquently in all areas of your life. It has changed my life, and I know it will change yours too.

Naked Presenting is You, Unplugged
Naked Presenting is not about being nude in front of an audience.

It's about being authentic, natural, the real YOU - the confident person who talks eloquently to friends without a script and without slides.

Your audience needs to listen to you. The way you tell it. With all the gestures and facial expressions and body language that bring your words to life.

Non-naked presenters hide behind things to distract their audience from looking at, listening to and concentrating on the presenter. They hide behind:
• A podium or a table – distancing themselves from their audience

- Notes or a script – a physical barrier, but one that stops them sounding natural or creating rapport with their audience
- Slides – so the audience looks at their slides, rather than the presenter

"You are everything your audience needs."

If you have already delivered presentations, then this book will help you to take your presentations to a new level. It will help you to share the very best of what you know (your Diamond), combine it with your natural personality, let your passion lose and create a Presentation that will Ignite your Audience.

If you have never delivered and want a simple, yet powerful way to learn how to take what you know and create a presentation, then this is a fabulous place to start. This process is simple and quick, saving you hours in deliberating and cogitating over what you could or should or need to say.

Novice or experienced, there are two secrets you need to now before you start:
1. You already know enough (about your topic)
2. You don't need anything other than you and something to say to ignite your audience

The most powerful impact you can have on your audience is to be present. Just you, no slides, no props, just you. Talking from your heart. Connecting with those listening in a way that is honest, authentic, vulnerable even.

The most flexible, most creative, most responsive, most reliable, most innovative element of delivering a presentation will always be YOU

You don't need to convince your audience to listen to you with a list of your credentials, by name dropping impressive clients or celebrities, by listing your awards and achievements. Most audiences are simply not interested. You need to simply deliver great value.

You can persuade your audience to listen by being silent. By waiting. By leaning in and whispering. By sharing a secret with them. By letting emotion into your words. Simple, powerful words delivered from the heart can keep an audience spellbound and leave them profoundly changed.

In ways that bullet points on a PowerPoint slide never have.

This book is not about creating 'PowerPoints'.

It's not about creating distance by hiding behind lecterns, having bold slides while you lurk in the dark. It's about paring down your presentation to its very essence, so that you can be heard, so that your words can be heard, so that your audience can feel what you are saying.

If you want to bore your audience with hundreds of dull slides packed with PowerPoint bullets and with your corporate logo on every slide, then this book may not be for you. Although your audience would thank you a million times if you read it and implemented it.

But if you want to create change, if you want to inspire others, if you want to deliver something so powerful your audience may remember it for the rest of their lives, then please read on.

<u>You</u> Can Ignite Your Audience
You may have never experienced a presentation that ignites an audience. A 'PowerPoint' has become short-hand for a presentation, as if there is a silent assumption that when you speak you must have slides as well.

Yet would Martin Luther-King's "I have a dream" speech have been better with slides? Did we even need to see Winston Churchill deliver his rousing call to action when he told us we would "fight them on the beaches"?

When you read this book, I invite you to think differently about presentations. To step back from what you have done or seen done before. To consider that there might be a new and better way to talk to groups of people. After all, what we currently know is that presentations are boring, have terrible slides and rarely leave an audience inspired, cheering and with an urge to go and change the world. Too often, presentations lack passion, lack soul, and worst still, lack really useful content.

Yet if someone can inspire me to walk over hot coals using just a few words, then what might you do if you knew the secrets of Presentations that Ignite Your Audience?

<u>You</u> Are The Expert In the Room

"An 8-year-old is God to a 6-year-old."

You do not need to have all the answers.
You do not need to be the most qualified, the most experienced person in the world when you present. Don't wait to speak. Don't wait to be acknowledged as an expert by someone else. You may never be ready. Your time is now.

Whatever your topic, you know amazing things – that can make a real difference to the lives of others. If you know a few things that the people in the room don't know, that is enough.

A business that is just starting out doesn't always want advice from one that has been around for 100 years. They want to hear from someone who is six months in. Someone who was recently where they are, who remembers the challenges and can give them some first-hand practical advice. You don't have to be Richard Branson to talk about how to run a successful business.

Redefine your definition of an expert. It is simply *"the person in the room who knows the most."*

Notice, the definition is not about the world, even

your country, just the room. You just need to know enough to be of value to those listening.

You need to believe that people want to hear what you have to say and that you have something that people need to hear. And I have yet to find a client who doesn't fulfil that last criterion, even if they need help in believing the first. Taking what you already know and designing an experience that creates a real buzz in your audience is not rocket science – if you follow the answers to the five questions in this book. Five answers to SPARK a Presentation that will Ignite Your Audience.

Imagine that you have just delivered a talk that really got your audience buzzing with excitement, believing in new possibilities, ready to change their world. Then days or weeks later, you get an email from them saying something like "your presentation changed everything".

Because in all honesty that is what this book and presenting are all about.

The Elephant in the Room!

Before we go on, let's just tackle one thing – those things that have been labeled *"Boring Topics."*

The truth is that there is no such thing. This is so important, I will say it again: there's **no such thing as a boring topic.** The fact that the presentation is boring is not the fault of the topic.

Some topics are complex - law, science, accountancy, for instance. But they are as jam-packed with interesting information and stories as the next topic. We just need someone to help us see that.

So if the problem is not with the topic, why do some presentations make you want to scream "you stole my life, I want it back" in the end?

The problem is not with the topic. The problem is with the presenter. Boring presentations are caused by one of the following:
1. Presenters who are bored about what they are talking about (and should just shut up).
2. Presenters who don't know how to make their topic interesting (who need to read this book).

If you decide your topic is "boring" then are you really going to search for the fascinating information in it and present something amazing to your audience? No, you have given yourself the ultimate excuse to not bother. You give yourself permission to put slide after slide on the screen packed with complex information that even you find heavy going. I have even heard presenters pre-empt their audience's reaction by introducing it apologetically with the words: "this is the boring bit."

Whereas the truth is more ordinary. Every single topic is **interesting** to someone...

And the person it most needs to be the most interesting to, if you want to create a Presentation that Ignites your Audience, is YOU, the presenter.

If Construction Law Can Be Exciting...
There I am with a 300 page Construction Law manual in front of me and I am not even a lawyer. A few months ago, I confidently bragged that I could make anything interesting and this is my biggest challenge yet. There is lots of jargon to unravel, lots of highly technical information that has to be word perfect. What have I done?

Using the SPARK provided by the answers to the most frequently asked questions on presenting, two lawyers and I developed and delivered a very unusual construction law workshop. It was Marmite. But we kept in mind this one thing: lawyers are human and they like to enjoy life too.

In the end, we delivered one of the most inspiring and exciting events the law firm had ever experienced. The audience loved it – they were involved, having a great experience, laughing and learning along the way. It was exciting, engaging and memorable. So good in fact that one lawyer said it was the 'best training course that I've ever been on!'

So what's your excuse?

Your Audience is King
While this book is about you, about you sharing your expertise with others, presenting is never about you. Presenting is all about your audience.

The most important person in the room is each and every member of your audience.

This book has been written with you in mind. It will be judged on whether or not you find it easy to use, on whether or not your presentations create a real buzz, on whether or not your audience starts talking about your presentations. The same will be true of what you say – it's not how entertaining it is, but whether it makes a difference to your audience that counts.

Your Biggest Questions Answered with SPARK
Here are the five most frequently asked questions about creating memorable Presentations...

QUESTION ONE:
How Can I Make An Impact Quickly? *Shareable Stories* are the fastest and most powerful way to make your topic come alive. Stories are easy to tell and one of the things your audience is most likely to remember and to tell others!

QUESTION TWO:
How Do I Know What to Say? *Pick Your*

Diamond. Your audience only needs to hear one thing of incredible value to think you are the best thing since the iPad. So find the ONE thing they most need to know – your Diamond – and leave out all the rest of the stuff you thought you could say. ONE thing they are dying to tell their friends, ONE thing that will ensure that you stand out from everyone else. ONE thing that will change their life.

QUESTION THREE:
How Do I Get My Audience to Remember Me Long After the Presentation is Over? *Awesome Afters.* Every single talk should make a difference to the people listening. They need to learn something relevant to their life that will make it better in the long term. Not masses of information, but 3-5 things that they can do differently can literally transform your audience and have a lasting impact on their life.

Question Four:
How Do I Keep Their Attention Throughout? *Remarkable Resources.* Your words, powerfully delivered can be enhanced, emphasised and brought to life with resources that make your audience sit up and pay even more attention to what is happening. But not just anything will do – they need to be remarkable!

Question Five:
How Do I Remember What to Say? *Know the Flow.* Hook their attention from your first words. Make them curious, eager to know more. At the end, create a powerful call to action. Knowing exactly how you are going to start and finish is good at tackling any nerves you might feel too.

Are You Ready to Ignite Your Audience?
This book, by itself, cannot change your presentations. Only you can do that. So at the end of every "how to" chapter, you will be invited to develop a presentation of your own, step-by-step on a topic of your choice.

In just a few hours, you will have created one of the most powerful presentations you've ever delivered. You will learn new tools and techniques that will save you hours and make your presentations more engaging, more fun, easier to remember. But only if you do something.

Recently I coached a client to prepare a presentation for a job interview. For a ten-minute presentation, we spent over 10 hours preparing what to say, designing a slide template to WOW them, 'Mining for the Diamond' in the presentation, and practising.

Was it worth it?
You decide: that job was a promotion that was worth £200,000 extra income.

Question One:
How Can I Make An Impact Quickly?

Presentations are notorious for being boring. Audience's wince as presenters stumble through slide after slide. Presenters drone on with no regard to whether or not their audience is even awake never mind listening.

The best way to keep your audience's attention throughout your presentation is to say less. But how can you still make an impact, how can you ensure that your audience leaves having experienced something profound, how will your presentation be remembered if you are saying less?

The simple answer is this: use stories.

Stories create memorable magic. Share a story and you bring your topic to life in a way your audience can grasp immediately. A great story will stay in their minds for decades.

Why Are Stories So Memorable?
Recent research by psychologist Jerome Bruner found that presentations containing a fact wrapped in a story were **22 times more memorable** than those containing the fact alone. Stories help your audience put themselves in the middle of the action – it's the closest thing to them actually being there.

When you present your audience with facts, their brains start questioning what they have heard. How many of you are wondering – where did I get that figure of 22 times from? It's our nature to be cynical and questioning. Facts can start debates in the minds of your audience that are counterproductive to their ability to pay attention and listen to what you are saying.

Stories have a very different effect: stories belong to the presenter.
While I have had people come up to me after a presentation and demand to know where I got my facts from, I never have (in 20 years of presenting) had someone question my stories.

Your Audience Loves to Share Your Stories
Stories are by their very nature viral. We love to share them – when you hear a great story, you think about who you are going to pass that story on to. We tweet about them, text about them and talk about them all the time.

A great story can have the entire room transfixed as everyone waits with bated breath to see how it ends.

Stories are far more likely to be shared at the end of your presentation than facts or lists, or your company's illustrious past. I regularly share the most powerful stories I hear during presentations. In fact, since I am very interested in the power of storytelling in business, I write down stories and then ask the presenter if they would let me share their stories with others. When I tell stories, I've heard from other presenters, I always credit the story back to its origin.

A few months ago I heard Steve Bustin, an expert in media and PR tell a story about an optician who had invented a new type of glasses. The optician had just 3 lines of copy (no more than an inch of space) in a national UK tabloid newspaper. As a result of that exposure, he sold out six months' worth of stock of his new product.

That story took Steve less than a minute to tell, but it had the WOW factor. I knew it was a story I was going to want to tell again, so I asked Steve if I could share it. He said yes, providing I didn't mention the name of the person. I've told that story at least ten times since hearing it.

There are four types of stories you may tell, which all need a different approach:
1. Stories of things that happened to you personally. You may wish to change the names of people who are involved in the story, especially if it reflects them in a bad light. I always ask permission to use people's names, even if it shows them in a good light.
2. Stories of things that you heard from others. Please ask their permission to tell the story first and always credit the story back to the owner. Never pretend that it happened to you or that it is your story.
3. Fables, stories of monks, metaphors, and

other stories. This is a common starting point for many stories in presentations. However, they can become overused. If you can, find stories that are genuinely unusual and that don't appear too often in other presentations.

4. Stuff you made up. Avoid this, unless you are a professional comedian. It is likely to come across all wrong. Anything that actually happened to you that you embellish beyond the point of recognition by other people involved in the real event falls into this category. Best left for fictional books or printed stories rather than telling in presentations.

Your Audience's Minds Are Open to Stories

Are you sitting comfortably? Then I shall begin... How many of you heard those words when you were a young child? We are taught at school to sit still and listen closely whenever the teacher told a story. We were taught to concentrate and listen. We were taught to focus on their words and the pictures in the books. We sat and listened intently and our attention span grew. Our ability to listen grew.

As a presenter, you can suggest things to your audience in story form that would create instant resistance if you just presented the same information as a statement.

A story invites an open, receptive mind. We listen to a story and then consider it.
A statement invites an inquiring, judgemental

mind. We question it, we accept or reject it.

Consider the following two approaches:

1. *Mary wasn't sure. Was her mole growing?
   Was it larger or darker than before? She asked
   her boyfriend. He couldn't be sure. Mary
   looked on the internet and ended up more
   confused than ever. What should she do? She
   decided it was nothing, then waited, to see if
   it changed. She peered at in the mirror. But
   she didn't really know what she was looking
   for. When she finally went to see the doctor,
   her first words were "if only you had come
   sooner"...*

2. *If you have a mole and it changes, go to your
   doctor.*

The first version is longer and takes more time to
tell. But your audience can immediately relate
to it. They imagine themselves as Mary, they
can imagine themselves looking in the mirror,
brushing it off as not important. They can
imagine how they would feel if their doctor said
"if only you had come sooner". They may have
even had a very similar experience. Without a
clear ending, they have to fill in the blanks for
themselves.

The second version is concise. But it is also lacks
connection and emotion. It is forgettable.

Your Audience Will Remember Stories

Twelve years ago I listened to around twenty presentations lasting 30 minutes on a University course I was taking. I can only remember ONE of them. That presentation contained a powerful story that surprised me and moved me to tears. Now, 12 years later, I can re-tell the story I heard about a charity that helped people who became blind later in their life. A story with one of the most astonishing final lines I have ever heard. The presenter, Sharon, told us the story of Edwina, who had become blind. She was initially scared, isolated, frightened. But after the charity helped her, Edwina's life was so much better afterwards that she said these unforgettable words "I wish I had become blind years ago."

WOW!

That story has sat in my brain for 12 years. Yet the other presentations I heard that night, and hundreds I have heard since, have left no lasting impression on me whatsoever. Edwina's story brought 100% of my attention at that moment and it was as if everything else stopped.

And it was my **emotional reaction** to the story that made it memorable.

If you feel something when you are telling a story to your audience, the chances are that they will feel it too. When you tell a story with emotion, with feeling, then you trigger something called *Mirror Neurons* in the brains of your audience. If your story that starts with you feeling frustrated,

your audience's brains light up in the region that
is associated with frustration. They are coming
on this journey with you and their brain is all in
for the ride.

When you tell a story that is uplifting, a story
of hope, for instance, your audience leaves
feeling hopeful and inspired.   A few years ago I
was working with a UK national cancer charity,
helping them to deliver presentations that ignite
their audience. Jane was a smoking cessation
specialist and wanted to inspire more people to
give up smoking.

Jane told an uplifting story of hope about a
smoker who used to lie on his sofa, surfing TV
every evening because he was simply exhausted.
He watched his young children playing and he
really wanted to join in, but at the end of a long
day at work he simply didn't have the energy to
do it. He desperately his life to be different, to be
a better dad, but he didn't know what to do about
it. With her help and support, he managed to
quit smoking. A few months later, not only had
he quit smoking but he had lots more energy.
He played happily with his children after work
and they were delighted. In fact, he had so much
energy that he ended up walking the entire
coastline of Wales, raising money for charity.

How much more impact does a story like that
have, over a statement like "quit smoking,
you will have more energy at the end of the
day"? People can relate to that end of the day

exhaustion, or to feeling that they wished they had more energy to play with their kids.

How You Can Check if This Is True for You
If you look back over your own life, the experiences that you can remember as if they were yesterday, are those where you had a very emotional experience. When it's almost as if the rest of the world stood still and there was just you and this moment. You can remember exactly where you were stood or sat, which room you were in, what time of day or season it was, and what happened.

Emotion is a trigger that stores things into our long-term memory. We are hardwired to remember those things that made us react emotionally because our lives depend on it.

So think about your own life – do you remember the things you bought at the supermarket 10 years ago? Probably not, because it didn't really matter and you had no strong emotional reaction to going shopping. So what are the things that you remember? Did you feel a strong emotion at the time?

My own autobiographical memory easily highlights experiences where I felt tremendous emotion - when I had my first kiss, when I got my Ph.D., the day my boyfriend asked me to marry him, and when my son first uttered the phrase "love you mummy".
Stories Make Presentations Easy to Tell

Stories make your presentations easier to deliver too.

Think of a well-known story, something like Goldilocks or Cinderella. Unless you have young children, you may not have read that story in years. Yet you could probably tell that story right now, without any notes.

Does it matter if you get every single detail right? Not really. Does it matter if you can't remember whose porridge was hot, or which bear's seat was too hard? Not really. Would it matter if you use a pineapple rather than a pumpkin when the Fairy Godmother creates a carriage for Cinderella to ride to the ball in? Not at all. What matters to your audience is the journey that the hero experiences. From rags to riches (Cinderella) or the adventure of Goldilocks exploring the bears' house.

When you tell a story as a part of your presentation, whether it's a story about your own life, or about someone else's life, you simply need to ask yourself:

"What is the key message of the story that I want my audience to hear?"

Providing you communicate the one thing you want them to remember, it doesn't matter if you tell the story exactly the same each time. Which means that you don't need long sets of notes. You don't need a script. You simply need to remember the core message and tell your story. You may find that your entire notes for that part of your presentation are just one word or phrase, such as "Steve Bustin."

Stories Help You Finish on Time

One of the things that my coaching clients often worry about when they are presenting is timing. They want to know exactly how long their presentation will last, because they know how important it is to their audience and/or the conference organiser that they finish on time (if not slightly before).

Novice presenters sometimes believe that a solution to that is to write out their script word for word. And I do NOT recommend it. Unless you are being inaugurated as the President of your country and it is vital that your presentation is word perfect, scripts should be avoided at all costs.

Another solution is to practice. To practice the whole thing several times and time your delivery, to measure how long it takes. Many presenters will take slightly less time on the day that they do in practice because they tend to speed up a little in front of an audience. I definitely recommend that you practice (see later).

Another even more flexible solution is to include stories in your presentation. Because you can easily make stories longer or shorter to suit your timing.

It is not unusual, particularly at conferences, that other presenters overrun their time slot (one of the worst sins of any presenter). So your planned 30 minute presentation suddenly becomes 15 minutes. Now because you will have Picked Your Diamond, you know exactly what you need to say most. You also have some stories to bring your topic to life that you can easily shorten.

Conversely, if you suddenly have twice as long because the next presenter has yet to turn up, you can put more detail into your stories and take it slower. It is really that simple? Consider the Cinderella story, for instance. You can tell the Cinderella story in several hours – as Christmas pantomimes around the world do every single year. And you can also tell the story in less than a minute.

Stories are one of the most flexible time elements of your presentation. Meaning that you get to finish on time, every time.

The Story Your Audience Loves to Hear
Your audience loves most of all to hear about themselves. They want to hear stories that resonate with their own lives, with their own challenges, with the problems they face and the opportunities that they hope are right around the corner.

As you start to use stories in your presentations, keep notes of them. Not necessarily in detail, but headlines and core messages. The more stories you have to draw upon, the better your presentations will be. When things happen to you in your life that create any strong emotion; from frustration if your train is late, to beaming when you get customer service that is beyond your wildest dreams, then take a few minutes and write it down. You never know when that story might be simply perfect for this audience and this topic.

Jonah Berger researched what makes a story go viral, by looking at the stories that people share with others. He started looking at which newspaper articles drew his eye, then researched which stories people shared using social media like Facebook.

His research has important implications for presenters who want their audience to share the stories they tell in their presentations. These two things make people want to share a story:
1. The story was positive
2. The story was exciting

So if you put all three elements together, then one of the best stories to tell your audience is an uplifting story about someone just like them that is exciting.

What I call a Cinderella story. A rags-to-riches story that resonates deeply with your audience and gives them hope that they can overcome their challenges, that there is a brighter future within reach. And not just slightly better, but considerably better.

This type of story is extremely powerful when you want to influence others to take action. In this case, you can use the following three-step format:
1. The struggle – where the hero started, which is very similar to where you audience is now
2. The resolution – how your hero's life is better now
3. The call to action – what the hero did to get from struggle to success (with the implication that they can do it to)

Take Joanne, for instance. She was a bookkeeper and she didn't know how to talk about her business. She dreaded networking and thought that people just glazed over when she told them she was a bookkeeper because it was boring.

I coached Joanne to tell stories instead of focussing on her products and services. Joanne tells a Cinderella story instead. She talks about a small business, where Diane, one of the partners, was spending two days every week pouring over the figures, entering data, doing VAT returns, and hating every single confusing minute of it. Joanne did the same books in just half a day a week, freeing up Diane from this dreaded task. This meant that Diane was not only happier but also able to spend more time with her clients and growing her business.

Her audience (typically small businesses) can

relate to that story. Anyone who is spending time doing their books and hating every minute of it will be nodding their heads thinking "that's me!". If they also then think "I would rather be happier" or "I would rather be spending time with my clients" then the call to action is implicit. They need to hire Joanne.

Stories are Powerful
Stories inspire us with what others have done and make us wonder if we could do that too.
Stories make information come to life in a way that facts and statistics never can.
Stories create powerful images of a possible future that can effortlessly change the way we act.
Stories engage our emotions, and emotions are key to remembering what you said.

If you tell a story about someone in your audience, you put the focus squarely on THEM. They realise that you care about them, their problems, and what they want to know.

How Do You Tell A Story Your Audience Can't Wait to Tell Others?
* **Talk about real people.** You can talk about the dangers of smoking, but meeting someone who is in pain and unable to breathe because of their smoking converts dry data into something very real and very human. When you use a human character, please give us their first name. It makes all the difference. "Mo did" is much better than "A man did."
* **Use simple stories.** The more complicated and

detailed you make your story, the more chance you have of getting it wrong or forgetting bits. If it's easy for you to remember, it's easy for your audience to remember too, so they are more likely to share it.

- **Tell vivid stories.** A story that contains something surprising or vivid is more exciting to share. What's more interesting – a story about a dog or a story about a tiny purple elephant that sits in the palm of your hand?
- **Feel the story.** Emotion helps us remember things, so if you include excitement, sadness or other emotions in the story, your audience will be more involved in the story and will remember it for longer. The longer the story stays in our brains, the more likely we are to share it.

Anne was a probate (wills) lawyer on one of my workshops and told a story about a client of hers. This woman contacted her in some distress having just lost her father. What was worse was that her father had taken out a loan, countersigned her name to it (without her knowledge) and put the family house up as collateral. She believed that her name on the document meant that not only had she lost her father, but the debt would have to be paid and she would lose her entire inheritance, including the family home. The lawyer fought the legitimacy of the loan in court and won. The client was delighted that Anne had managed to save the family home. Before she told me that story, I had no real idea what a probate lawyer did, or why I might ever need to use one. That story was uplifting and gave me goosebumps. And I remember it over five years later.

How You Can Tell a Powerful Story Quickly: Lucy, the Handcuffs, and the Key

There are only three things that you need to tell a simple story:

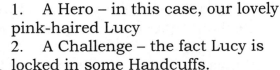

1.   A Hero – in this case, our lovely pink-haired Lucy
2.   A Challenge – the fact Lucy is locked in some Handcuffs.
3.   A Resolution – how Lucy gets out of the handcuffs

Some things that people think are stories are in fact just anecdotes. Stuff that happened that is not a story, and, therefore, unlikely to be interesting enough to hold your audience's attention.

For instance:

"I went to the shops and bought some milk."	Not a story. Hero ✓ Challenge ✗
"I went to the shops and then discovered my purse was missing."	The start of a story - Hero ✓ Challenge ✓ With a problem now in place, it just needs a resolution and then it's done.

As humans, we are inherently problem-solving beings, so we thrive off problems. It is why people love detective stories and mysteries. Your audience is also curious. They cannot hear the start of the story without wanting to know how it finishes. You can use that yearning to find out how the story ends to keep them hanging on your every word.

Why not start a story near the start of your talk, then tell your audience what happens next near the end?

Empower Your Audience, Make them The Hero!

If you really want your audience to be as involved as possible in your story, then it's powerful if they relate closely to the hero in your story (in this case Lucy).

You want them to hear about their trouble or situation and think "that's me!"

✓ If your audience is all male, you might want to rename your hero to be Luke instead!
✓ You want them to relate closely to the problems Lucy is facing, so choose a story where the

handcuffs are similar to problems they are facing in their lives right now.
✓ You want them to mentally cheer when the Lucy gets out of her handcuffs. You want them to think: "that could be me."

When I was working with Birmingham University's Cancer Research Department, we worked on telling stories as part of their fundraising. If you are a charity who wants people to donate to you, whether that is time or money, stories about the difference they will make to individuals is a very powerful motivating force.

Which of these is more likely to have you reaching into your pocket to help?
If you donate money to us, our charity will print more leaflets about the signs and symptoms of cancer and distribute them to households in your area.

Peter has just been diagnosed with bowel cancer. He has a son, Billy, who is just 4 years old and a new-born daughter Emily. Your donation will help us to distribute leaflets that might help people like Peter notice the early symptoms of cancer sooner. So Peter might not have to go and tell his wife and family that he needs an operation and they will have to battle through cancer..

The Challenge, Problem or Opportunity

What is it in the life of your hero that is getting in the way of them being happier, healthier, wealthier or more fulfilled?

There are six themes that tend to crop up when you are telling Cinderella style stories:
1. Money – being in debt, having too little income, having too many expenses
2. Time – feeling rushed, not having enough time to get everything did, not spending time doing the things you really love
3. Safety and Security – feeling that you can relax because you have a job that is secure, or a solid foundation for your business
4. Looking Good – not just physically, but being recognised for your contribution, having prestige, having a brand that is recognised
5. Feeling Good – having energy, passion, enthusiasm, and self-confidence
6. Stress – frustration, relationships, work/life balance

These themes can be useful as you reflect upon the story you want to tell. Which of these themes is the most important to your hero?

You can then develop the story further, with these questions:

1. How **intense** is the pain or problem? How much do they recognise that it is a problem in their life? How willing are they to find a solution? It can be hard work to convince someone to listen to you if they don't recognise that their problem actually is a problem.

I was coaching a business owner to tell stories about his business. Brian ran a photography business and wanted to convince other businesses that they should use their own bespoke photos on their websites instead of stock photos. However, he struggled to prove what a difference it would make to their businesses. He *knew* that it was important, but without the right story, without the right information the people he was talking to simply did not see that there was a problem, so did not buy his solution.

2. How **urgent** is the pain? How important is it that the problem is solved either NOW or soon? The more urgent the pain is to your hero (and potentially your audience) the more willing they will be to listen to your story, and the more they will want to hear your solution/ the ending to the story.

One of the most powerful ways to engage your

audience in your story is to use their own exact words. If you can talk to your audience before your presentation; either by arriving early or talking on the phone a few days beforehand, you can ask them some questions to find out what they are feeling and thinking.

When I tell Joanne, the bookkeeper's story, I use her exact words "she dreaded networking". That means that other people who feel the same will relate to it in a way that if I paraphrased it by saying "she didn't like networking" would not.

You want your audience to be able to relate to your hero. So while it can be helpful to use the same gender, if you add too many details, they might decide that are not the same and ignore the lesson contained within. If you decide your hero is a 45-year-old woman with a business employing 5 people, then solopreneurs or larger businesses might dismiss the story as irrelevant. The fact is that it doesn't matter if Cinderella is 21 or 41, blonde or dark, Caucasian or Japanese. What matters is her journey.

If you say your hero was struggling to make ends meet, more of your audience may relate to their predicament than if you say they had run up credit card debts of thousands of pounds by gambling.

The Resolution or Solution
Conversely, when you are talking about the solution, or how your hero's life is so much better

now, if you're precise and exact, you can create a more powerful desire for your audience to take action.

You do not want your story ending to be vague or fluffy. A phrase such as "she had more money" could simply mean she had another penny in her pocket. You want to say "she paid off her debt in just 3 months and now has nearly £10,000 in savings." That is tangible, specific and people will really connect with the ending.

You want your audience to say to themselves "I want that" or "I want to be your hero". Because that is when you create momentum for them to change their lives, to take action, to put your advice into practice.

How to Give Your Story Even More WOW
There are three ways to enhance your story:

1. **Make it Urgent** – take Lucy in her handcuffs. If you add the Houdini element so that she is underwater and has to get out of the handcuffs before time runs out, that adds urgency to the story and makes it more compelling. Time is a common way to add urgency – *"we had to solve it by midnight or we would lose the sale."*

2. **Make it Seem Impossible** – the harder, or more intractable the situation seems, the more your audience will be surprised when the resolution arrives. A classic "impossibility" element is

money. *"We had to build the house in just 4 weeks and we had no money at all to do it, not even a penny to our name."*

3. **Make The Stakes High** – when the outcome is high stakes, then it automatically creates more interest. *"We had just one hour to make a meal"* is not that exciting, until... *"to impress the buyers and show them how our catering service was the one for their new chain of hotels."*

Make Your Story Come to Life
There are a few things you can do when telling your story to make it come to life in the minds and hearts of your audience:

Name Your Hero
Whenever you can, name your hero. Giving your hero a name changes your story from fiction to fact. If you are tempted to amalgamate various stories into one and give your hero a made-up name, beware! Your audience will quickly pick up on the fact that the story is not wholly true and it will have far less impact than one true story. Not only that, but you will start to confuse yourself.

Create Pictures in the Minds of Your Audience
Earlier I told a story that Jane, a cancer cessation specialist, told me about a man who gave up smoking. When Jane first told the story, she simply said, "he lacked energy."

There is no clear, definite image that comes to mind when your audience hears a concept phrase such as "little money", "low energy", "business was hard". You need to make it easy for your audience to SEE what you are talking about:

Concept	Picture
Little money	She was hungry. She vainly opened the kitchen cupboards, hoping that this time there would be a tin of beans hiding at the back. She was heartbroken when she realised that there wasn't a scrap of food in the house and it was still 3 whole days to payday.
	He opened his wallet at the checkout and was embarrassed to realise that he would have to put either the milk or bread back, as he couldn't afford both.
Low energy	He crawled out of bed in the morning, exhausted and wondered to himself yet again, "how am I going to get through another day?"
	She wanted to go the gym on the way home. She'd promise herself she would, every morning for the last 3 weeks, but she just didn't even have the energy to get changed into her workout clothes, never mind pound the treadmill for

Business was hard	30 minutes.
	She looked at the figures and realised that in the last 3 months she had barely made minimum wage yet was working 15 hours a day on her business, every single day of the week. She was beginning to think she would be better off working on the checkout at the local supermarket. In fact, she knew she would be better off, at least financially.

He looked at the order books and thought – if something doesn't happen this month, then I am going to have to let some people go.

One of my clients, Tess, was presenting at a higher education conference on the topic of student engagement. The entire topic initially appeared quite conceptual, so we talked for some time to get to the real heart of the message and make it about people. In the end, she told a love story in the style of Romeo and Juliet (except with a happy ending), of the students falling in love with the city of Leeds and the city falling in love with its students. She had an incredible reaction from the audience and the conference organiser was quite emotional by the end, and over the moon with Tess's presentation.

Your Story is Not a Book
Most stories in presentations need to be quite

short. Between a few minutes and ten minutes long. Expert storytellers can continue for longer but only with practice and skill. The shorter your story is, the easier they are for you to tell, and the more likely the story is to be shared.

Too many characters and your audience might get lost or confused. Too many details and they might struggle to keep track of what is going on and where they should be focussing.

How You Deliver the Story Makes All the Difference
Learn how to vary the tone and pace in your voice when telling a story to make it more realistic and memorable

In developing stories about cancer with a national cancer charity, we chose to develop a story about bowel cancer where each of the two presenters would take on a character and tell their story, with the two stories interlinked. The two stories were based on the fact. Each person started with the same symptom and one of them went to see their doctor and got treatment and the other did not. Gradually the one who did not go to the doctor went quiet and stopped talking. It was a graphic illustration that made a great impact on those listening.

Time For You to Tell A Story
✓ Select a presentation topic that you have already spoken on, or one that may be coming up the in the future.

✓ Think about the audience you are likely to present to – who are they? What do they already know? What are their ages, genders, job roles?

✓ Brainstorm a few stories that you could use to bring the topic to life, keeping your specific audience in mind

✓ Think about what you want your audience to feel at the end of the story – Hope? An urgency to act now?

✓ Draw two images (stick figures are fine) that portray the start and end point of your story – starring your hero of course

✓ Tell the story out loud a few times, while being fully aware of what you are feeling. If you don't feel something while you are telling the story, what else do you need to say or is there a better story?

✓ Tell the story to a few peers or friends and see how they react. Read their faces closely as you tell the story. Are they nodding, smiling, frowning at the right moments (a sure sign they are connecting with the content)? Then ask them afterward what they felt.

✓ Tell the story as part of a presentation and then follow-up perhaps a week later with a few of the people who were present. Do they remember the story? What did they learn from it?

Question Two:
How Do I Know What To Say?

You know a great deal about your topic, in fact probably too much to squeeze it all into the time you have to speak. Presenting is not about showing off and showing how much you know. In fact, one of the quickest ways to bore your audience and leave them overwhelmed is to cram in far too much information.

If your audience wanted to know everything you know, they would pick up your book and read it.

The more you tell your audience, the more they have to remember.

Not only that, but as the presenter, the more you want to say, the more YOU have to remember. So you'll need more notes, more practice, and much more time to prepare.

This "cram it all in" style of presenting is also known as the "spray and pray" approach – where the presenter sprays information at their audience and prays that some of it will stick.

Yet the truth is that your audience doesn't want

or need to hear everything you have to say. What they really want is the next step or two on their journey.

The workshop was entitled "How to market your business." My business was fairly new and I was already confused about what I should be doing, so I went along with high hopes of getting some solid advice to help me move forward. In 45 minutes, the presenter gave me hundreds of extra ways in which I could market my business – from articles in the local paper to giving talks, to social media. I left with a huge list of things to do, but also rather demoralised. I had wanted someone to simplify this minefield, not add to my confusion. Needless to say, I did nothing. Her presentation was packed with *information*, most of which I already knew or could have researched on the internet. But it created no transformation - it had no lasting impact on my business or my life, except to serve as an example of what NOT to do.

People need transformation, not information.

How Your Knowledge Can Be a Curse
You may know a lot about your topic. You may have spent years learning about it. If you have, then you could probably talk about it for days. You may have what is commonly referred to as the **Curse of Knowledge.**

The result of this curse is that you know too much to cram it all into your presentation, but you aren't clear what to put in and leave out. As the expert, you need to work out what is the most important, the NEED-to-know advice for this audience. You need to forget all that you know and try and remember what it was like before you know what you know now. How can you make their life easier by sharing what you have already learned and mastered?

Experts need to take complex things and make them easy. If the speaker at the "how to market your business" workshop had taken me through a simple process of writing an article and then advised me how to get it into my local paper, that ONE piece of practical "how to" advice would have had immense value. I probably would be thanking her right now for how it changed my business and my life. I would be singing her praises – and I would be telling you her name. And I am not.

Focus Your Content From the Very Start with a Diamond

One of the most powerful ways that I have found to create a presentation is to start by finding the Diamond in it. Your Diamond is a piece of advice so valuable, that if your audience remember only that one thing from your entire presentation, they will have had tremendous value. They will leave feeling that listening to you was worthwhile. Their lives will have been changed.

Your Diamond needs to be unique to you. It needs to be your specific advice, your specific opinion on a topic. It should not be common knowledge or a trite saying that pops up on Google every other day.

The most important piece of advice in this book is this: stop trying to tell them everything and start sharing your Diamond with your audience. Your Diamond will make your presentation shine.

How Does Sharing One Diamond Make a Difference?

Firstly it makes you more confident when you present.
That confidence comes from knowing you are sharing something that will make a real difference in the lives of your audience. You know your Diamond is brilliant and your presentation clearly delivers it. Your Diamond is something you already know has made a difference in the lives of others – maybe even in your own life.

It means that even if you only talk for five minutes, you can give your audience tremendous value. You can shorten your talk if you are asked to, and you know exactly what needs to be said and what can be left out. However long, you have, you know the one thing you need to share: Your Diamond.

Secondly, it makes preparing your presentation much faster.

As someone who is easily fascinated by information, I used to agonise for hours over what to say in my own presentations and workshops. I could spend hours researching the latest news or tips, and end up with so much information I could have delivered for days. It was only by developing my Mine for Your Diamond process that my presentation preparations stopped taking over my life.

Sarah Fox of 500words.co.uk found that when she picked her Diamond, her preparation time for her interactive workshops on construction law was reduced from one week to just one day!

If, like me, you find yourself agonising over what to say and what not to say in your presentation, your Diamond will give you instant focus. As one of the first steps in preparing your presentation, you will never need to create and then delete a PowerPoint slide again. Because you haven't even opened your computer at this point. Not only that, but you will only research additional material if you feel there is something missing.

Thirdly, your presentation becomes more powerful.

When you Pick Your Diamond, you focus on your audience. On what your audience most needs to know. Not what you want to say, nor on the best stories to tell, nor on what statistics is going to WOW them, nor on how to impress them. You focus clearly and simply on what your audience most needs to learn right now.

So, if you start getting presentation-creep and thinking "should I add this?" you simply look at your Diamond and ask yourself – "does this point, story, anecdote, slide or statistic support my Diamond or not?" If it's not directly relevant, you can leave it for another presentation.

Finally, you get to shine.

Your Diamond is the very best of what you know.

The very best information that this specific audience needs to hear.

So if you Pick Your Diamond and focus your presentation on it, your audience will love your presentation and you even more.

Why More is Less: The Paradox of Choice
Barry Schwartz, in his fascinating book "The Paradox of Choice" tells a story about selling jam. He talks about whether having more or less choice increases sales of jam. The research compared the amount of jam sold in two different circumstances. In one, customers have 6 types of jam open that they can taste. In another, there were 24 types of jam to taste. Paradoxically, the greater the number of jars of jam you were

able to taste, the fewer likely customers were to buy. About 30% of those given just six to taste purchased jam. But only 3% when they had more to choose from. Why is that?

Because the shoppers were overwhelmed by the decision. They can pick their favourite jams from 6, but not from 24. So if they feel confused, if they feel unsure about whether the decision they are making is the right one, guess what? They don't choose at all. They would rather not buy jam than buy the wrong one.

How does this apply to your presentations? The more options, tips, hints, advice or possible avenues of action you give your audience, the less likely they are to act upon it. It's back to the marketing speaker again. With hundreds of choices of ways to market my new business, I remained confused and chose none.

People are not starved of information. In our own pockets, on our smartphones, our computer or in our libraries we can quickly and easily access almost any amount of information on any topic we choose. I could have spent 45 minutes researching "ways to market your business" just as easily as I could have gone to hear the speaker present. As the speaker then, you need to bring something new to the table, to guide people through the maze of options available. To help them choose which jam to buy. They need to know, out of all the options available, which one you recommend they do next.

The most important thing for you as a speaker is to choose, so your audience doesn't have to. Just choosing the most important next step for them is an act of great service to your audience. People are hungry for certainty, for simplicity, for practical advice. Give it to them.

How Your Diamond Helps to Ignite Your Audience
Your Diamond brings clarity and focus to your presentation. It will stop you going off at a tangent, and keep you on track as you are presenting. For anyone who has a tendency to ad-lib and just go with the flow, and who subsequently tends to overrun when they are presenting, having a clear singular focus can help you keep to time.

How many times have you heard a presenter say "I could talk on this topic for years, but we only have…."? The things are, your audience doesn't care how long you could talk, they only care that in the time you have, that you are going to share something that is valuable to them. Your Diamond helps you sift through everything you could say and highlight which ONE thing you are going to share in this one presentation.

When your presentation is over, you want to be able to go up to anyone in the audience and ask them "what was the most powerful thing you learned today?" While, each person, is likely to take away slightly different things, if they all say variations on a theme, then you know that your Diamond gave clarity and focus to your content.

Your Diamond helps your content to shine. When your content shines, it will make a lasting impression on those listening. That means that your audience is most likely to remember what you said, hopefully for years to come, and, therefore, act on your advice.

Your Diamond clearly tells your audience **why** they need to listen to you. It is vital that you answer the question that they are all thinking: "What's In It For Me?" Your audience needs to know why they should listen to you, rather than update their Facebook status, or skim through the hundreds of emails that are piling up in their inbox as you speak. Your audience needs to know why they should even turn up to your presentation, rather than do something else, from tasks in the office to shopping. You need to let your audience know that they are in the right place and that they will learn something potentially life changing that they will value.

A client of mine, Judy Parsons, was preparing a short presentation for a social media event as part of Wakefield Business Week. As author of the Solopreneur Guide - "Link Up with Linked In", she had more than enough expertise and knowledge. Her position as part of four presentations on other social media outlets meant that she needed to quickly demonstrate why LinkedIn was important to businesses – the WIIFM aspect. We found her Diamond and presented it using just two slides. The first had a photo of a phone and Judy asked them to Google their name and business. She then presented a screen shot showing that her own LinkedIn profile came top of the Google search results, before her own website. It clearly demonstrated that if your clients are looking for you, that your LinkedIn profile needs to be given the same care and attention that you give to your own website.

Why One Diamond Is Better Than Lots of Bling
- One Diamond will help you focus on the most valuable information you have to share
- By cutting out the bling, your Diamond will shine more brightly
- One Diamond makes it much easier to remember what you need to say
- Your Diamond will make an invaluable impact on those listening in a short time
- You'll spend far less time preparing (it takes just a few minutes to find your Diamond)

How to Mine for Your Diamond
If you remember just one thing from this entire book, then this one process is it. Diamond mining is the opposite of Death by PowerPoint. This will focus your content, ensure you share something of real value, cut out the clutter and make your presentation super quick – all in one simple process.

Are you ready to get clarity and focus? Are you ready for what you say to shine? Are you ready to let go of some of what you know and leave it for another presentation?

Step 1: Mine the Ground
– here you are digging
up every single thing
that you could tell your
audience. No judgment.
Just brainstorm
anything and everything.
Write each idea on a
separate piece of scrap
paper or Post-It note.

Keep going until your desk is covered in small
notes and ideas. You may look at them and
instantly identify things that are missing. You
may think "that is really two things". Make sure
that each note is a single idea – not a topic such
as "benefits", but a statement such as "having a
Diamond saves you time". It can be helpful to
have someone else do the writing while you allow
ideas to come to mind, as writing can be the
slowest part of the process.

Step 2: Keep Digging – as with mining real
diamonds, it's vital not to stop too soon. You
never know when the next shovel-full might
contain a **Diamond**. Keep going until you can't
think of another thing. Keep refining your ideas
and thoughts. Keep getting clearer about the
ideas behind the ideas. Keep going. In most
instances, this process is complete in just a few
minutes. For very important presentations or
where you have a long time to prepare, you might
put your notes on a whiteboard or wall and keep
adding to them over several days.

Step 3: Sifting – it is now time to start judging your ideas. Not on whether or not they are important, or if it took you a long time to learn it. If you think like that, then you will find it harder to let go. This is about stepping into the shoes of your audience. Stepping back from all this information you have mastered through sweat and tears, and going back in time. Back before you knew all this. You need to look at these ideas through their eyes. That will make this process easier and faster and stop you hanging onto things for dear life.

It's time to dazzle your audience with fabulous information. It's time for you to sort the rubble from the gems. You need to be utterly ruthless. You are going to edit out anything that does not need to be said, anything that your audience doesn't desperately NEED to know right now. Look through all your notes and decide: which of these ideas will literally transform people's lives? What does my audience most NEED TO KNOW?

Your goal is to throw out the things that are obviously not Diamonds until you only have a few shining ideas left.

Two Methods To Select Your Gems – 1. Follow Your Instinct
This is the fastest way to find gems amongst all the ideas:
• Look at all the ideas you have (if possible spread them all out in one place such as on a table or the floor) and then read them

individually.
- Bring to mind your specific audience for this presentation
- Quickly crumple up any that you think are not powerful or the next immediate steps and throw them out of reach. By crunching them up, they are no longer a distraction and you can concentrate on what is left.
- Keep going, eliminating options and notes until you only have a handful left.
- The important thing here is not to have to justify your selection and to act quickly.
- You may find it helpful to have someone help you with this step

Two Methods To Select Your Gems – 2. Winner Stays On
This method can either be used from the very start, or when you have already eliminated some ideas and need to choose amongst those that are left.
- Again, keeping your specific audience in mind, take two ideas at a time. Pick them up and compare them. You can only keep one.
- Which of them does your audience most NEED to know?
- The other one that is not as strong for this audience is crumpled up and thrown away
- Pick up another idea, and compare it to the winner from the last pair
- Keep comparing just two ideas at a time until you are left with one or a few that you cannot choose between

Step 4: Choosing the Brightest – for each remaining idea, consider the impact it will make on this specific audience. Keep the one that will make the biggest difference, and disregard the rest, however much you love them. You may even ask your intended audience. Always remember, however, that you are the expert. You know what worked most powerfully and you need to be your own counsel in many respects. Sometimes audiences think they want to learn something and yet you know they need to learn something else.

Your Diamond should be specific, simple and powerful, as well as passing the "so what?" test (see below).

Tess was due to speak on "Embedding Student Engagement in the Curricula" at the RAISE conference to hundreds of people from higher education. She had around 30 different ideas when we were Mining for her Diamond. Ideas on structure, involving the community, the benefits of the students, the university and the local people, and the importance of external collaboration. She went on to say how it improves, employability, feedback on the projects that had been delivered, student learning logs and finally the importance of a buffet. Yet one of them, leaped out from the rest. One of them was powerful and had a real emotional hook. The idea was this "to help the students fall in love with Leeds." When we reviewed that as the Diamond for her talk, all the other important information was reflected in that Diamond while others became less important and were easily thrown away. It became the basis of a superb story that had her audience entranced.

Step 5: Admire Your Diamond. Now you have ONE amazing Diamond in front of you, let go of all the rest for now. Admire the one you have and appreciate it – it will make your topic come alive!

Check Your Diamond Passes the So-What test?
As presenters, we can become too close to our own material. So it's now time for a sanity check.

Share your Diamond with someone who is either going to be in your audience, or is similar to those who will be in your audience. Don't say too much, just share your Diamond and see what response you get.

Do they seem interested, in a *"Wow! That sounds amazing, please tell me more"* manner, or politely disinterested, aka *"that's nice"*?

How to Know if Your Diamond is Fake
There are a number of simple tests that you can perform on your Diamond to ensure that it is a genuine Diamond and not a cheap fake. Ask yourself these questions:

Is your Diamond NEW?

If you say something trite, something that people have heard before, then your audience will stop paying attention. They will presume that you have nothing new to say. And once they have decided that, you have lost their attention and it is very difficult to get it back.

One of the most over-used quotes about public speaking is "people are more scared of presenting than death." It is not new information. People have heard it before. It's not even true. Another one is to imagine your audience naked because that will get rid of nerves. These phrases are bound to have your audience rolling their eyes and going straight to their phone to tweet about how boring and predictable you are.

Check if your Diamond has already been used by searching on the internet. If there are lots of results that have your exact phrase in them, you might want to be more creative, or take an alternative point of view.

Is Your Diamond RED?

One way to grab your audience's attention is to say something that is the direct opposite of what they might expect to hear.

One of my coaching clients was preparing a keynote speech for an audience of project managers and wanted to get across the point that most big construction project failures are the result of lots of smaller things going wrong, rather than the more easily anticipated big things. We came up with this phrase "Failure is Your New Best Friend". When everyone working on risk in project management is looking to avoid failure and design it out, she was telling them to embrace it. It became a very tweetable quote that made her talk shine.

Is Your Diamond UNIQUE?
I was working with some business women, helping them refine their Diamond so that their elevator pitch, or 60 second business summary at a networking event would stand out and help them be remembered. They had all been Mining for their Diamond, to find the one thing they needed to say.

One lady confidently volunteered her Diamond. She said, "I help you fulfill your potential." While that seems a powerful phrase, it is also overused and predictable. What is worse is that it pretty much summed up everyone's business. From a bookkeeper who does your books and helps you spend more time serving clients does, to a coach, a graphic designer, a web designer, a printer – everyone, in fact. Needless to say, her Diamond does not pass the "so what?" test.

Time For You to Pick Your Diamond
✓ Turn back to the topic you chose earlier when you selected a story.
✓ Now think about your audience again.
✓ Brainstorm all the things you might tell them about your topic.

✓ Use the processes to select the ONE most valuable thing that you think that specific audience needs to know about your topic.

✓ Share your Diamond with some people who are similar to or from your intended audience. Does it pass 'So-What?' test?

✓ Check that your Diamond is not fake, by verifying that it is New, Red, and Unique.

✓ Now go back to your story. Does it fit with the Diamond you have now chosen, or would a different story suit your Diamond better? Make sure that any stories you include will enhance and reiterate your Diamond, rather than side-track your audience's attention.

Only once this step is complete can you move onto step 3... Moving forward before this step is complete will make your entire preparation so much longer and more iterative than necessary. Get clear now and you will save hours later.

Question Three:
"How Do I Get My Audience to Remember Me Long After the Presentation is Over?"

Your Diamond is the foundation of a presentation that will give tremendous value to your audience. Yet it is just a powerful idea. Your audience craves the skills and knowledge to solve their problems or to perform at a new level.

Your Diamond is your focus, but you need to deliver something that will last long after your presentation. You are going to convert your Diamond into some very practical, tangible takeaways or **Awesome Afters.**

Awesome Afters

If your presentation is to be the antidote to *Death by PowerPoint*, then you need to make a lasting impact on your audience. You need to create a transformation in their life. You need to be able to set a goal for your presentation with a measurable outcome. After all, if you are not intending to change people, to make their lives better, then why even present?

So returning to my client's keynote with the surprising focus on "Failure is your new best friend", it was not enough just to give them a catchy tweetable phrase. She also gave them four practical tips, which spelt the word STAR, to ensure that they avoided the most common ways that construction projects fail.

Taking this book as an example, it is important that you recognise the benefits of having a single clear Diamond in your presentation. That fact is just information. The book will transform your presentations when you practise how to Mine for your Diamond so that you experience the power of the Diamond for yourself and can do it. The Diamond Mining process is something you can use time and time again. That will make a real difference to you, saving you literally hours of preparation, while helping your Presentation to Ignite Your Audience.

Your Awesome Afters Are the WIIFM Factor
As mentioned earlier, your audience needs to know before they even arrive that they are going to get value for the time they spend listening to you. They need to know "what's in it for me?" – aka WIIFM.

If you can take your Diamond and then translate that into three to five real benefit statements, written from your audience's perspective, then they will clearly understand why they should turn up. It will tell then why they should listen, and what sort of a difference you will make to them.

Think about your life as if you were a member of your audience. What is their life like? What do they worry about? What would they like more of in their lives? How will your Diamond help them?

There are two main ways in which your presentation might impact their lives:

1. **Reduction in problems or pain** – how will these skills reduce negative experiences such as stress, frustration, debt, costs, time wasted, feeling tired all the time, coughing for England?
2. **Increase in solutions or gain** – how will these skills produce positive experiences or improve their life – more time, more energy, more income, better health, more quality sleep, living longer?

Now dig a little deeper. What other impact will those situations be having on their lives? Take the example that someone is tired all the time. What is the impact of that? Could it be that:
- They don't have the energy to get a job
- They don't play with their children or grandchildren
- They are grumpy and their relationships aren't as happy as they would like

The most important thing is to talk to your audience using their own words. Saying something like: *"Would you like to maximise your return on the property market"* it's not the same as *"Would you like to retire with plenty of money from the sale of your house?"*

If your presentation title clearly explains WIIFM, then your audience are more likely to turn up or watch it online. If your presentation invitation or outline lists a number of practical and tangible takeaways, they will not only turn up, but be eager to listen to you and curious about what you are going to say.

You Are Taking Your Audience on a Journey

Think of your presentation as a journey – you get to take your audience from where they are now to somewhere new. You get to decide how far to take them (and how fast you will travel) and where you will end up.

The journey may be a short hop or an epic exploration, depending on how long you have to talk and how long it takes to give your audience the confidence and information they need to take that next step.

You have to Know Where You are Starting From
It is **impossible** to define an *Awesome After* for your audience, if you don't know where they are starting from. If I asked you for directions to London, UK you couldn't possibly tell me anything useful without knowing as the bare minimum:
•   Where I am starting from
•   When I need to be in London

You might also want to know other information such as what is my budget? if I am travelling with others, and any specific requirements I might have. So if I have three weeks to get to London and I am starting in Paris, France, then there are

a range options available. As the expert in the
room, you get to present a few tried-and-tested
options. You might decide that low-cost is the
most important thing (your Diamond), so you talk
about how to safely hitch-hike to London or how
to raise the sponsorship for a bike ride to London.
Your Diamond might be that travelling itself
should be a luxurious adventure, so you could
talk about the most exclusive ways to travel from
Paris to London.

If your presentation is a journey, and your
expertise is helping knowledge experts to get
their work published as a book, there's no point
talking about how to find a publisher if the
audience is full of people who only have a vague
idea if they even want to write a book.

You need to get to know your audience. You need
to know things like:
- Who are they (age, gender, number, job roles,
  dreams)?
- What problems do they have?
- What opportunities can they see ahead?
- What do they already know about your topic?

Imagine your topic is time management. If
your audience is busy working mums who
are juggling children with running their own
business working from home, then your content,
your stories, your Diamond,and your Awesome
Afters would be very different than if you were
presenting on Time Management to teenagers
studying for their exams, or CEOs who were

managing multiple staff and projects at once.

You may simply be able to ask your audience, they may be your peers, colleagues or managers. But what you think might be their problems or opportunities, might not be the same as what *they* think they are.

NEVER *assume your audience is like you.*

Whenever and wherever you can, you need to find out about your audience in advance. It is far better to spend time researching your audience, that researching your topic.

How You Can Get to Know Your Audience
1. Ask the organiser of the conference or the meeting about who they expect to be in the audience.   If you get specific names, research those people online, you might find useful insights on social media, on blogs, on their comments and posting that give you valuable information about them.
2. Ask them directly, for instance with a survey. When I have been presenting workshops in new organisations, I often ask if I can survey the participants beforehand. When I suggest that this will help me to make the workshop more relevant and more valuable to those attending, many organisations are only too willing to help. You can ask questions to individuals over the phone, which is ideal but time-consuming, or send out a survey using a website like SurveyMonkey. Not everyone

completes the survey, but the information you will get from a short survey of only 6-8 questions can be invaluable. Not only that, but your audience will love to hear the results of the survey too. It makes your presentation all about them. They love that.

3. Research the organisation or host. There is so much information available online regarding organisations and individuals, there is simply no excuse for presenting without knowing something about your audience.

4. Talk to them at the venue. If you are presenting as part of a conference, then arrive as early as you can (at the start of the day, before anyone else is ideal). Talk to the organiser, talk to the tech guys, talk to the attendees. Find out everything and anything you can. Listen to the other presentations and make notes. It can be very helpful if you mention things people said during your presentation, such as "Mike from accounts told me that...." It shows you care, it demonstrates your understanding of their specific situation and everyone who knows Mike perks up when they hear his name.

5. Ask the audience during your presentation. As a last resort, you might even ask questions of your audience to guide what level of detail you discuss various tools or techniques.

6. Observe your audience as you present. If you are making your topic too complicated for them to follow, then the energy in the room will drop. People may start to fidget, or whisper, or use their phone. You need to be

able to respond to your audience so that you know that they are still engaged and learning.

Once you are crystal clear on who your audience is, you get to develop material that is a precise fit for your audience. It is easy to decide what goes in your presentation, and what to leave out. I call this the "guest list" approach to presentation preparation. You start with your Diamond. Then you develop a list of some Awesome Afters. They become a filter (or guest list) for what you include in your presentation.

Every single story, every single question you ask, every exercise you develop, everything you ask them to write down, every word you say needs to clearly and directly relate to your Awesome Afters. If it is not on the guest list, then it doesn't get in.

How to Write Your Awesome After
The easiest way for you to write your Awesome Afters is to think about your audience, focus on your Diamond and then complete the following sentence: *"By the end of this [presentation, workshop, seminar, course], you will be able to...."*

What comes next has to be a verb. A doing word. Because the only thing you can truly measure as an outcome is something observable, something you can see people doing. Here are some verbs that are most commonly used in creating Awesome Afters:

Create	Select	Evaluate	Reduce
Compare	Define	Analyse	Explain
Investigate	Perform	Summarise	Identify
Describe	Design	Compose	Plan
Develop	Calculate	Modify	Write

When you are writing your Awesome Afters, chose only those that will literally transform the lives of your audience. Keep your focus on practical value rather than clogging up their minds with more stuff.

Why Your Awesome After is Never About "Understanding."
A presentation is about change. Not about information. Presenters sometimes use fluffy phrases that fail to clarify exactly what their audience is going to learn. They say the objective of this session is to help you *understand* more about [their topic] Or to "increase your awareness of.."

How would you know that I understood *more* about Health and Safety?
What exactly do you want me to know – the date the Health and Safety Act was first passed in parliament? How to exit the building safely if the fire alarm sounds? How would you even know how much I knew about your topic before I came into the room?

A presenter was having trouble getting good feedback on her talks and I offered her some free help on her evaluation forms. They were so vague. She asked her attendees to mark various statements using tick boxes labelled with titles such as "exceeded my expectations". I asked her "what if you audience expected to be bored rigid? Would exceeding their expectations be a good thing?"

Vague objectives that include the word "understand" help neither the presenter to decide what to teach the audience, nor the audience to know why they need to be there in the first place. Not only that, but it is impossible to measure the impact of your presentation.

Synonyms for "understanding" that are also to be avoided include: know, knowledge, comprehend, awareness and appreciate/appreciation. If you want to ignite your audience, then don't set an objective to improve their appreciation of anything!

Describe instead exactly what you would **see** or **observe** your audience being able to do, given this new "understanding". For instance, if they understand more about how important it is to market their business, would they:

- Create a simple marketing strategy?
- Set aside a monthly budget for marketing?
- Decide on ONE marketing strategy to implement consistently over the next 90 days?
- Stop doing marketing that is not proven to bring in new customers?

Examples of Awesome Afters
When I wrote this book I had six Awesome Afters

in mind, and they were written as follows:

By the end of reading this book, you will be able to:

1. *Tell a simple story that your audience will really want to share with others*
2. *Select the one thing (the Diamond) your audience really needs to hear*
3. *Define what you want your audience to be able to do after listening to you*
4. *Design at least two Remarkable Resources that will enhance what you are saying and bring it to life in a way that makes your audience go WOW*
5. *Deliver powerful bookends for your talk that will help you relax and present with confidence, while hooking your audience's attention at the start and inspiring them to action at the end*
6. *Structure your presentation so that it flows effortlessly from the powerful beginning to the call to action at the end*

Whenever I was wondering what to write next, or whether the idea I had in mind was relevant, I could return to my list of Awesome Afters and clarify if the content fitted my plan or not.

Taking Awesome Afters to the Next Level

You may have a topic which is very specific or has to meet certain legal or internal standards for training. There are three additional elements that you can use in defining your Awesome Afters.

1. Quantification – how many. If you were presenting on marketing, you might have an

After that says that they will "select the three most important marketing strategies to suit their own business". If you were teaching the capitals of Europe, you might want your audience to be able to "list at least 10 of the capitals of the main countries in Europe".

2. Standards – how well. For instance, if you were presenting on business communication, your After might be to "Write a business email containing zero grammatical or spelling errors". Your After might measure how fast they can do something, or that they create an elevator pitch that gets them a WOW!

3. Context – when/ with whom/ in what conditions. If you present on business networking, your After might be "To identify at least one person to follow-up with at every single networking event you attend." That After also contains quantification (one person). You could even add a standard, such as "follow-up within 2 days of meeting them."

Developing Your Awesome Afters into Your Outline
With a story, Diamond and some Awesome Afters, you now have enough information to start planning out your presentation in more detail. Start to fill in a summary of your presentation, with the following information on it:

Your Talk Title	This needs to be engaging, specific and to hook the audience's attention before they even arrive (see below)

Date and Time	The day of the week has an impact on your audience, as does the time of day. Are you presenting just before lunch after several other presenters, or just after a heavy lunch of sandwiches and cake?
Duration	How long is your talk going to last – you might want to note the range (perhaps if you are speaking at a conference)
Audience	How many, who are they?
Room	What is the room layout – are you at the front, on a stage, with a microphone, where is your screen so you never turn your back on the audience?
Technical Stuff	How do you deliver your talk – do you need to bring a USB, send the slides, access your Dropbox over a WIFI? Do you control the slides or the tech guys? Do you have a microphone or not?
Your Diamond	What is the ONE thing your audience NEEDS to know that you must keep in mind throughout the talk
Your Awesome Afters	What will your audience be able to DO by the end of your presentation? Three to five points depending on the duration of your talk

Your Remarkable Resources	Any resources that you wish to bring with you – from a banner advertising your business, to slides, to music, to props (see Remarkable Resources)
Your Opening Line	What first few sentences are going to hook your audience's attention and have them putting away their phones to listen intently (see Know the Flow)?
Your Closing Line	What is the final line you want to deliver (always AFTER a Question and Answer session) that is a gift to the audience? Something to inspire them, something you want on the tip of their tongue when someone asks them "what did they say?"
Your Intro	What you want the host, the MC (master of ceremonies) or the compere to say to the audience as they introduce you and your talk to the audience. Prepare this in advance, send it to the host, and also bring a large font sized copy with you to give to the host in case they have lost it.
Your Outro	What you want the host, the MC (master of ceremonies) or the compere to say to the audience after you have spoken. See comments under Intro.

If your presentation is going to last longer than 15 minutes, then you will need to develop a more detailed plan. One way to do this is to create a timeline or storyboard. A detailed example that I developed when delivering a one-day workshop on the SPARK presentation process is shown. This is the first page and was used primarily in the design phase rather than the delivery.

Under Remarkable Resources, I included notes about which page in their Workbook (WB) they might need to use.

NAKED PRESENTING			**CLIENT NAME**		
Course Diamond(s)	You have Diamond information that will Transform the lives of your audience, and you need only that Diamond and yourself to create a real buzz				
Awesome Afters (by the end of this workshop you will be able to…)	1. Tell a simple story to inspire your learners to action 2. Mine for Diamonds to select N2K information 3. Create clear and measurable Awesome Afters 4. Describe four learning styles and how to support those learners best		5. Analyse ways to embody your company's brand 6. Explain how to modify your content to suit your audience 7. Deliver a powerful opening to a presentation 8. Prepare and use one method for keeping track when presenting		

Time	Story	Pinpoint	Awesome Afters	Remarkable Resources	Know the Flow
		The Diamond / Emotion	Involvement - Actions	Learner/ Facilitator	Open/ Close/ Link
	Arrive			WB/ Diamonds/ Slides	
09:30		Create a buzz... / Curious	Use words from invite/ survey monkey		
09:35	See it, believe it	/ Excited	"this day would be an amazing event if…"	Flipchart and pens	
09:40	Say hello	Which was easier to remember?	In pairs – share for one minute. One talks about themselves. One shares a story. In fours, introduce the other (30 secs) Which was easier?		Link: you've told me why you are here…
10:00	Story [Sue]	/ Inspire			Open: The story we want you to be a part of
10:05	Impact of 3 stories	Five minutes can make a difference	A well-told story can make an impact in just five minutes!		
10:10		Naked is You: Unplugged			
10:15		Focus on one presentation / Reflecting	Complete the boxes on page 2 – which presentation to which audience	WB p2	
10:20	Transformations	Tell a story to inspire others to action / Engaged	A story on your topic - about how that information has already changed one life	WB p3	Link: What's the biggest mistake presenters make?
10:35	Paradox of Choice - Chutneys	Too much info = no transformation / Confused	Review poster and determine what is the most important piece of information present Compare results!	CR Attributable Risk Poster	
10:45	Mini-Break				
11:00	Mining For Diamonds	Select Need to Know information / Engaged	10 mins brainstorming them all 10 mins selecting the ONE	Post-It notes WB p4	
11:20	Fruit Salad Semi-skim Milk	Transforming Objectives	Which of these is great TO? (5 min) Create TOs for your topic (10 min)	WB p5	
11:35	The Planets	WIIFM / Humbled?		WB p6	
12:00		Blinky the Fish			
12:05		Map Emotions / Enlightened	Emotional timeline Where did they start/ finish?	WB p7	
12:20	Lunch				

For a short presentation, you need far less detail. However the key elements are as follows:
1. Summary box at the top – with the Course Diamond and the Awesome Afters
2. Then a time structured plan with the duration split into segments and notes alongside.

When you first practice your presentation, you can then make notes of your timings and see if you need to adjust your plan to ensure that you finish on time.

Your Title Should Let Your Audience Know Why They Should Listen to YOU
In a world filled with choices, your talk title needs to grab your audience's attention and make them want to listen to you. Whether your presentation is live, on YouTube, via webinar, you are competing with hundreds of other speakers or other things your audience could be doing with their time. So you need to give your ideal audience enough information in your talk title for them to choose to listen to you.

As a presenter, you might think your first impression is when you start to speak. But you make an impression when the person reads the advance notice of the presentation. You make an impression when they walk in the room, when they first notice you, when you greet them, when they listen to your introduction, when you walk onto the stage.

By the time you start to speak, you have already made at least five impressions on your audience. Five chances to excite them about your presentation, five chances to connect with them personally, five chances to influence them with your confidence and poise, your knowledge and expertise.

One of the very first impressions you make upon your audience is with the title of your presentation. Something they are likely to read days, if not weeks before you speak. Your title needs to grab their attention and make them eager to know more.

You want your audience to arrive eager to listen, curious to hear what you say and fully attentive. A great title will do just that. Paired with a set of Awesome Afters, your presentation will be irresistible to the people it is most designed to help.

What You Can Learn From 4000 Presentation Titles
To distil best practice in creating powerful talk titles, I researched over 4000 titles from over 700 speakers. It was an eye-opening experience. And it taught me that many presenters find it hard to write a great talk title. Many use fluffy titles that are really just a general topic.

You can tell if your title is actually at topic using this simple test: does the library have it listed as a category? Presentation Skills is a topic, not a title. Similarly Leadership, Management, Conflict Resolution, Change Management, Marketing, Sales, Health, Work-Life Balance, Motivation,

Innovation are all topics. They are huge areas. They are not suitable as titles for a book, never mind a presentation.

Some of the titles were topics in disguise or topics with extra bling. Additional words of phrases that made it seem different, but had NO real value to the audience in helping them know if the talk about be useful to them.

Adding dynamic words or phrases alongside a vague topic does not make it better. An example is: "Presentation Skills for the 21st Century." Now the 21st Century started a long time ago now, so it's not that relevant and this is just a topic in disguise. It would only be useful if other presenters were offering a different course, such as "Presentation Skills for the 18th Century".

Another approach is to add adjectives to their topics, such as "Effective Presentation Skills". Yet since no-one is offering a talk entitled "Ineffective Presentation Skills", this remains just as vague.

Your title needs to talk directly to your audience. This specific audience, not all audiences ever. Ideally it wants to clearly define the content and give people a reason to think "I need to hear this". If you have already identified the pains your audience wants to solve, why not use that in your talk title?

One of my favourite talk titles from Courtney Anderson was this:

"If my title says manager, why do I feel like a babysitter?"

It is a fabulous talk title. It's funny, so you imagine her presentation would be funny. When I read it again, I rolled my eyes, because it felt like she was talking directly to me. I used to feel like that when I was a manager. This title created an instant connection, a rapport with the presenter. If you are feeling like that, do you think that the presenter would have some valuable answers to your problem? Of course, you would because she clearly understands your situation. It says so in her title. It is also memorable. I read it once and it stuck.

Note Courtney's presentation is not entitled "How to manage difficult people" or "Delegation 2.0". Those might be the topic of her talk, but her title has a clear and specific Diamond in it. It speaks directly to organisations and individuals who are experiencing this exact problem.

A few years ago, I created a short presentation on how to write titles. So I had to prepare a title of my own that would grab the attention of those who most wanted to watch it. This was the result (the presentation can be found at authorstream. com/nakedpresenting).

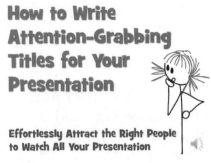

How to Write Attention-Grabbing Titles for Your Presentation

Effortlessly Attract the Right People to Watch All Your Presentation

NOTE: Great titles are rarely short. If you really want to draw people in and make them curious, then fewer words are not better.

I once created a presentation for lawyers on presentation skills. The title my co-presenter and I developed was this: "How to Prepare Powerful Presentations the Night Before You Speak and Still Have Time to Sleep". Yet the organiser changed it to "Powerful Presentation Skills". Their revised title failed to clearly explain that one of the key aspects of the workshop was that people would learn how to prepare a presentation in record time. Something we knew that our audience needed to be able to do and would therefore be attracted to.

Awesome Afters – Diamond TakeAways
- If you want your audience to leave buzzing, you need to give them the skill or knowledge to DO something that they didn't know how to before they arrived at your presentation. If you have the right Diamond, then what they can do afterwards will be valuable to them and make a real difference.

- It is better to concentrate on a few (3-5) Awesome Afters that you know will make a real difference in their life, than creating a long list of information you only have time to skim over. What you want to do is give them core skills that create such an impact they will tell all their friends and colleagues about it.

Time For You to Create Awesome Afters

✓ Working with the same presentation, now develop your Diamond into between 3 and 5 Awesome Afters.

✓ Ensure that you can observe and measure each one. Think about how you might check to be certain that they can do those things at the end of your talk.

✓ Test these on your intended audience – find out if they would really value being able to do those things.

✓ Create a plan or storyboard for your presentation based on the examples provided above.

✓ Craft a title for your presentation that focusses on the difference you will make to your audience, or on the problem you will help them solve.

Question Four:
How Do I Keep My Audience's Attention Throughout?

One of the most predictable things that happens when people prepare a talk or presentation is that they open their computer and start up some presentation software.

Yet in this process, it is one of the very last things you need to do.

Why?
Firstly, if you start using PowerPoint straight away, you have already decided that your slides are your core focus. However Presentations that Ignite Your Audience focusses on the words you use, the skills you give people, your Diamond and your story. And you don't need a computer for any of those elements.

For centuries, man and womankind have managed to influence small and large groups of people without a single slide in sight. The power of their words, their charisma, their clear ideas, their philosophy, their beliefs changed people's lives forever. Jesus, Winston Churchill, Martin Luther King, Ghandi, Nelson Mandela: none of these leaders used slides. Yet they inspired nations.

Secondly, if you open up your

computer, there is much less chance that you will deliver a highly creative, innovative talk that includes pulling a rabbit out the hat, if only because there isn't one in PowerPoint!

Thirdly, most of the time that is wasted in developing presentations is the mind-dump approach where presenters create lots of bullet points and slides before they have even decided what to say. So they create slide after slide after slide, and then they talk to someone and realise that everything they have already done is all wrong. So they delete it and start typing in new slides.

Let's go back to our trip to London, UK. Opening up your computer and typing your thoughts onto slides is rather like setting off in the car and driving without looking at a map or the road signs. You will spend hours getting lost, using up fuel, and you can end up further from London than you were when you started.

You Don't Need a Computer to Develop a Presentation that Ignites Your Audience
If everything you are going to say is on your slides and in your handouts, then why are you there? Just give your audience your slides, let them read them and ask them if they have any questions in the end. You are not a narrator. You are a presenter. That means you have a fantastic opportunity to give your audience something truly valuable. You get to focus their attention in a new way, challenge their beliefs, give them

something that is potentially life-changing.

Resources must enhance your words. They do not replace them or substitute for your presence. Your presence is fundamental to a presentation. Your tone, your body language, and your delivery can change the very meaning of the words on your slides. So every single thing, from the room layout to the lighting, to the posters, or invitations that accompany your talk needs to be selected to add real value or a new dimension.

Every resource is subject to the **Law of Diminishing Astonishment.** If your audience has seen that quote 1000 times already, they switch off. If they have seen that photograph 100 times before, they are disinterested. You will have to be creative if you want to hold and keep their attention with your resources and words.

In the 1980s, PowerPoint was unknown. Presenters used slides – actual photographic slides in a carousel to illustrate their talks. Or they used an overhead projector with printed transparencies. In the 1990s, when PowerPoint started to get better known, computer slides were unusual, rare even. In the 2000s, stick men, bean men and clipart made slides more visual.

Then came the era of Presentation Zen, when having full-screen photographs from stock photography was the norm. Time marches relentlessly on. What seemed unusual last year can be old hat by the end of this one. If you want your audience to stay awake, if you want to engage your audience, if you want them to remember your message, you need to create **Remarkable Resources.**

Things your audience have not seen before. Things that are unique to you. That's why I invented Lucy, my stick figure. It became faster to draw an image I wanted than to find one (cheaper too). She also began to be part of my brand. My brand was about paring things down to the essentials, and Lucy is about as basic a figure as I could get away with. She helps me to bring my content alive in a way that stands out and she is instantly recognisable as mine.

If Your Resources Aren't Remarkable, They Are Forgettable
When it comes to making your message come alive, you have to find and use REMARKABLE resources if you want them to be remembered.

Predictable = Boring = Forgettable

Slides with text or bullet points are instantly forgettable. They wash over us like another episode of Midsummer Murders. Quotes that have been used a thousand times are forgettable – who cares?

Several years ago, while working with some health care presenters, they showed me a resource that I will never forget. This yellow lump represented just one pound (half a kilo) of fat.

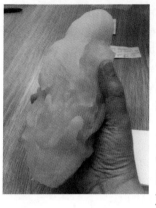

Really? WOW!

I was so impressed that I took the photo on the left. I tweeted about it. It was remarkable.

How powerful is that if you want to talk about weight loss or health? Whereas your audience might think that losing one pound of fat is not worthwhile, if they felt it in their hand, and thought about losing it from their waistline, or from their organs, they would have a more visceral reaction.

Apparently they come in five pound versions too. I almost wanted to have one to put in my fridge, to remind me what five pounds in weight actually looked like.

A presenter called Stuart Harris once used a Kerplunk Funnel in his presentation on customer service. The sound as the marbles (clients) fell out of the funnel onto the floor was something I still remember years later.

Resources that Are Instantly Forgettable
When you are designing your resources, **remember** that it doesn't matter if you have never seen or used something before, because it is your audience, not you that decides if your resource is Remarkable or not. This is particularly true for PowerPoint novices. If you are in any doubt, read

the list below or ask a few people. This list is not exhaustive and new things are added every week:

- Animating your words, slides, or images or even individual letters. Just because you found a new thing that PowerPoint can do, doesn't mean you should use it.
- Clip art and cartoons – where have you been for the last 20 years?
- Stock photos of people looking bored during a presentation – where have you been since Presentation Zen was published?
- Bullet points – it doesn't matter how clever your bullets are, they are still bullet points. And as everyone knows, guns don't kill people, presenters with bullet points do.
- All and every single built-in slide background and template in PowerPoint. Leave them alone. Please.
- Clashing or rainbow colour schemes. Unless you are presenting a talk about rainbows to toddlers, then leave the 1970s colour schemes alone.
- Unusual (and mostly hard to read) fonts. Chiller might look exciting on the slide, but it is still just words and unless your theme is something like the Best Scary Movies of all time, leave it alone. Not only that, but the chances are that your unusual font will be changed to something like Arial when you get to deliver it.
- Graphs or charts that are pasted directly from Excel into the slide, without taking out all the inessential items.
- Anything 3D – especially 3D pie charts (that

distort the data), or line and bar charts (ugly and unnecessary).
- All Word Art (see rainbow above).
- Lots of irrelevant Smart Art – such as using cogs to visually describe how different departments in your organisations need to "mesh" together to be effective.
- Any text that has been copied wholesale from another document and simply left as sentences and paragraphs.
- Bangs, whistles, zooming, flying, and other weirdness. And that includes horrible slide transitions too. Just stop it right now. Prezi users beware – those transitions have a tendency to make your audience feel seasick.
- Printing your slides as handouts (see later)
- Writing something on a flipchart – although if migraine-inducing slides are the alternative, it is a vast improvement.
- Videos – especially well known corporate ones that are not bang up to date
- Any photograph that is grainy, out of focus, badly composed, low resolution, or tiny on the slide
- Bean men

So What is Remarkable?
Now that you are banned from using most of the functions in PowerPoint, you need to start thinking about things that are remarkable. And bear in mind that the more people use any of these resources, the more unremarkable they become. So you have to keep reinventing your approach, your resources and being creative.

Extremes of Size Can Be Remarkable

Is big always remarkable? Not if it's just a slide projected large – unless it was over the entire front of a building perhaps. It would need to be something huge and unexpected.

If you are presenting a topic on change or risk, then you might use a die or dice. Having small dice in your hands that you shake together is okay, but imagine the look on your audience faces if you suddenly bounce a large inflatable die into their midst and watch as they push it into the air. Could that be remarkable? Yes. Providing it directly supports your Diamond and your Awesome Afters.

I once spent an hour or so creating a huge colourful target on a white cotton sheet. When I wafted it out and laid it on the floor, it definitely caught my audience's attention.

Conversely small can be remarkable too.
Most business cards are boring. When I started giving out small glass diamonds, as well as my card, people suddenly started begging me for one! Remarkable is just that – something to make us remark about. People still talk about my Diamonds years later.

At an event, I was talking about the importance of strong visuals. I said, "Think of an Elephant. No, not one like that. A tiny purple elephant, standing in the palm of your hand" – I held out my right hand to illustrate the point. "A tiny purple elephant that is blinking at you. She trumpets loudly and dances around, tickling your hand". A tiny purple elephant in the palm of your hand is an image that will be remembered. Think of Seth Godin's purple cows. Now you would need to be turquoise striped zebra to stand out. Purple cows are old hat.

Texture Can Be Remarkable
Most presentations contain no textures at all. So anything fluffy, silky, leather, diamante, dazzling, shiny, soft, squidgy or tactile in any way will stand out. People love touching things and having things they can hand around. When I talk about problems during presentations, I use a pair of diamante handcuffs to illustrate the point. People remember them.

That said, it doesn't always work: I remember sitting through a presentation on the (then) new chip and pin machines. Even the machines failed to make the presentation come alive.

A friend of mine, Lee Jackson, the PowerPoint Surgeon talks about slides being a crutch for the presenter. He brings out a crutch when he says that to enhance the point he is making.

Taste or Smell Can Be Remarkable
Have you ever considered the aroma in your presentation?
You can buy small fans to distribute smells around the room when you are presenting.
Venues can often smell musty or stuffy, so having

a burst of citrus smells, which are meant to enhance concentration, can make the atmosphere more pleasant.

But why not consider deliberately creating a bad smell? It could work, depending on your topic, and providing you can easily replace it with something nicer and it doesn't hang around.

Dark Can Be Remarkable

As presenters, we can work hard to ensure that there is sufficient light so that our audience can see us. After all, they need to see our facial expressions and body language to read what we are saying.

But what if you delivered part of your presentation in the pitch black? I once delivered part of a lecture in total darkness. I wanted my audience to focus on music and using music and their voice to enhance their presentation. So we closed the blinds and turned off the lights. Later on, I used a simple hand-held torch to illuminate my face while I talked. It was powerful and memorable session for all involved.

Sound Can Be Remarkable

Sounds, music and sound effects can all have an impact on your audience. A whistle can be startling, the sound of the sea can be soothing. Whilst you must check that the venue has the right licences to allow you to use music, music can be a powerful way to alter people's emotional states, to get their energy pumping or conversely to help them relax and listen intently.

Hand Made Can be Remarkable
For a workshop on Employment Law, I once
created fake cheque books. Each had around 10
cheques in them, and they were quite accurate
representations, with a tear off stub and all the
main features of a cheque book. During the
presentation, there was a quiz on employment
law. If a member of the audience got a question
wrong, they had to write out a cheque for how
much it might cost their company if the employee
ever took them to court or tribunal. It was a
powerful reminder of just what their ignorance
could cost them personally or their company.

Similarly, one of my clients used fake money, in
the same way. If her audience teams answered
questions on legal contracts wrongly, they were
fined an amount that represented the seriousness
of their mistake. She even had a red telephone,
so that if they would have to phone up their
liability insurer if they made a really disastrous
mistake. It was far more powerful and immediate
than just a cross against a question.

It can take only a few minutes to create
homemade wheels of fortune, snakes and
ladders, towers of bricks and all sorts when I
used to deliver training events. While they might
not suit your chosen topic and your audience,
the more creative you can be, the more your
presentation will Ignite your Audience. There
are also resources online, such as the Trainers

Warehouse, where you can buy similar items.

Emotions Can Be Remarkable
Typically our strongest, most vivid memories are
of events that were important to us, and that
created strong emotional responses in our lives.
In fact, our brains only transfer information
into long-term memory if we have an emotional
response to it. As the presenter, why not plan
the emotions you want your audience to feel, as
clearly as you plan the words you want them to
hear?

Some powerful emotions to consider are listed in
below:

CURIOSITY
Create curiosity in your
invitations or the title of
your talk. Or in your title
slide or posters around the
room. Get it right and you
can build a real buzz in your audience before you
have even opened your mouth. As you introduce
your topic, you have about 30 seconds to hook
your audience so that they are curious to learn
about the solutions to their problems. What's
the best way to get someone curious about your
topic? I'll tell you later....

EXCITEMENT
Your audience should arrive curious – if for no
other reason than to know how you will solve
their problems. Now you need to PROVE that

you can, and already have solved their problems albeit with other people. The best way to do this is with a Story. Tell them how your topic changed Mary or Mohammed's life. Make it real, make it tangible and create a powerful, compelling vision of how their life will be better (less pain, more gain) as a result of implementing the knowledge and skills they will learn at your session.

ENLIGHTENED, EAGER TO LEARN

Show your audience how they can change their own life. Enlighten them with surprisingly simple yet powerful tools or techniques that they can see are easy to use and will make a difference. Get the audience involved, by getting them to try things out in a safe environment. The more your audience is actively involved in the learning process, the more they experiment with the information and skill, and the greater their confidence grows.

REFLECTION, SUPPORTIVE

Every brain needs time to think about new information. They need opportunities to make connections between what they already know or have experienced, to the new information and integrate it into their brain. When your audience is asking searching questions, then they are testing their own understanding. It is a clear demonstration that they are really thinking about what this information means to their own lives. This time for reflecting is vital during your sessions, which is why breaks are so important – and it's also when you are most likely to have someone ask a great question!

CONFIDENCE, COMMITMENT
Learning will only transform your audience once they can apply the things you have taught them and feel confident in doing so. They also need confidence that these solutions are the right ones and will make an impact on their lives, which you can do by telling a story about someone like them.

Variety is Remarkable
If you want to transform your audience, then you need to have their attention. Research shows that an adult's attention span is just 10 minutes long, so if you are speaking for longer than this, you will need to create variety and change to keep your audience alert.

You can create variety by including:
• New stimuli such as a Remarkable Resource, a quotation on audio, an eye-catching or emotion-creating photograph

- The element of surprise to grab their attention (I once popped a balloon to show the impact of "no" on ideas)
- Stories, since the tone, pace and rhythm of a story is quite different to that of your normal presentation mode
- Questions or interaction (see below)

Involvement is Remarkable
Even if your audience is paying full attention throughout your presentation, they will remember little unless they are involved physically and emotionally. This table shows how little we remember of a presentation just two weeks later, depending on our level of involvement.

Action	Retention*	Media
Reading	10%	Books, handouts, journals, computer text
Listening	20%	Lectures, audio, and radio
Looking	30%	Charts, diagrams, flipcharts, whiteboards
Following	40%	Computer graphics, working models
Watching	50%	Videos, DVDs, demos, CD-ROMS, animation

Writing	60%	Reports, learning logs, tests
Talking	70%	Discussions
Practising	80%	Simulations, exercises, multi-media
Experiencing	90%	The real thing

*Retention is measured after two weeks.

If you stand and talk to your audience, they will remember just 20% of what you say. Yet a story that has them experiencing feelings can increase that to 90%. A simple way to involved them is to ask them questions to get them thinking about the information. If they talk to their neighbour, they are even more involved, and if at any point you can get them trying something out for real, then their retention will go sky high. Even watching someone being coached or trying something out is far more real and memorable than just listening to the theory.

Why Remarkable Resources?
- How often have you left a talk and rushed to tell your colleague that the presenter used something incredible – a bullet point? My point exactly!
- If you want to stand out from all the other presenters, then you need to do something different and that includes using resources that are new and different
- Mostly your audience should be listening to

you as you share your Diamonds and make a real difference. Resources of any kind should ONLY be used when they are more powerful, more memorable and more meaningful than words (which makes them REMARKABLE)

- Use props, images, video, photographs, charts only when they truly enhance what you are saying, rather than as something to distract your audience from looking at you
- Consider if your audience really needs to see your corporate logo and branding on every single slide you present. Will they really forget who you are if it's not on every slide? Surely having it on the first and last slide is enough – any more will not make your presentation any more memorable.

A Remarkable Makeover
In delivering presentation skills workshops, based on the five SPARK steps, I created an upside down pyramid that illustrated different levels of interaction that presenters can use during workshops.

While it was valuable to stimulate discussion, I decided it was dull and predictable. I called it The Interaction Pyramid™. Although why I bothered to TM it is beyond me, after all, it's boring.

So I set about making it remarkable. The shape was the trigger for some sketches and ideas. The upside-down pyramid suggested a cone. Before you know it, I went from cone to ice-cream and there was a clear match between the content and the concept.

After all, the ice-cream cone itself is fairly bland, then you add ice-cream, sauce, a chocolate flake and even a cherry on top. Hey presto, my boring Interaction Pyramid became The Cone of Plenty. It's more visual, more memorable and so much more interesting to talk about. And the audience love it, after all, who wouldn't want to talk about the "cherry on top"?

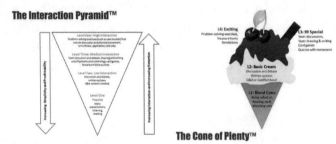

How many times have you seen a quadrant used to explain everything from time management to the client analysis? Is a quadrant inherently interesting? Is it heck! Yet time and time again, we use simple (yet boring) systems when we could be using something creative and innovative.

A Rant About Slides, Handouts, and Notes.
Point 1:
Too many presenters type their notes and script onto their slides.
Imagine going to the cinema and seeing the film script played in real time on the screen. You would be outraged, bored and would soon leave.

Your script is for you and you alone. Do not let your audience see it. Research shows that if you give your audience your words, their attention is split. They are neither listening to you, nor reading the text very well. So they remember even less that if you put the slide up and shut up. Leave words off your slides wherever you can. If you need notes to remember what to say, use index cards (numbered and either stapled or tied in order together).

Your slides are an opportunity to illustrate things that are hard to explain in words. Use them for large screen graphics, photographs, images that you don't want to draw on a flipchart or explain.

Why put words on them? They are NOT your subtitles for the hard of hearing!

If your slides make great notes to remind you what to say, they are LOUSY SLIDES

Point 2:
Just because PowerPoint or your Slideware programme lets you print your slides as handouts, doesn't mean that **you should**.

If your slides have fantastic visual images and photographs on them, then what is the point of printing them as handouts? You want to design slides that don't make sense without you being there to bring them to life, because otherwise, you might as well hand out the slides, let your audience read them, then when they have finished ask if they have any questions.

If your slides make great handouts, then they are BORING SLIDES

If you have strong visual slides, then you might print your Notes Pages as handouts. The strong visual image is at the top of the page, and beneath are some notes you type in separately or as you are developing your presentation.

The golden rule to remember is this:
Your Notes ≠ Your Slides ≠ Your Handouts

Time For You to Create Remarkable Resources
✓ Start with a blank piece of paper. Now thinking about your Diamond and your Awesome Afters, which things, stories, actions, concepts need a slide or image to help your audience grasp them? If none, great! Think of all that time preparing slides and checking you have the right USB stick and projector you have saved.
✓ There is no LAW that says you have to have slides. Some of the most powerful presentations I have ever seen were delivered without slides.
✓ What else could you add that would really get your audience saying "Oh" or "Ah." A video clip, a quotation, a large fluffy dice, some fake cheques, a crutch, a homemade Kerplunk Funnel? When presenting on the importance of having a clear idea of your ideal clients for businesses, I like to use the "Guess Who" game. It is a perfect illustration of the issue

and it is highly memorable.

✓ Use simple board game or TV game formats to create exercises that get your audience involved in your topic. Some of the simplest formats are easy to borrow from radio and TV quiz formats such as "Call my Bluff" or "Who Wants to be a Millionaire?".

Question Five:
How do I Remember What to Say?

One of the biggest fears when it comes to actually delivering your presentation is the fear of forgetting what you are meant to say.

By having a simple presentation format, by clarifying your Diamond so that your audience can easily remember the ONE thing they must take home with them and by designing a few Awesome Afters, you have already made your life a great deal easier.

You are saying less so that you have less to remember.
You have some powerful stories that demonstrate the value of your topic and its Diamond to your audience.

Yet even with all that preparation, a large crowd is still a large crowd. Your board of directors can still be a butterfly-inducing audience. Your promotion is still a situation that might have you a little bit dry in the mouth.

And there is a solution. You simply need to know the flow.

Know the Flow
Nerves do not disappear with a word-for-word script for your presentation. Novice presenters might want a script as a crutch, but your presentation will suffer if you read from a script.

For starters, your reading voice is not as nice to listen to as your relaxed, conversational one. Most people become stilted when reading a script, they struggle to follow the script, so stumble if they read it slightly wrong.

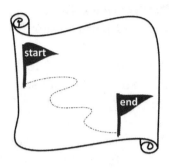

They are too busy worrying about reading than engaging with the audience, in responding to the room or being spontaneous.

Also the script gets in the way. You lack eye contact with the audience, and it becomes a very obvious physical barrier between you and your audience.

Many years ago, I watched as a student presented from her script. However she was incredibly nervous, possibly more than usual as her presentation was being assessed. Her nerves made her hand shake. Her script then amplified that shaking and became an even more noticeable sign of her nerves. Not only that but she found it hard to read the script because it was moving about so much. The whole audience was distracted and uncomfortable watching her struggle.

Unless you have to be word perfect and have lots of time to practice until you are natural and get it right every time, please avoid using a script.

Most presenters are more likable, more natural and easier to listen to when they ad-lib. And I do not mean total stream-of-consciousness here. You have already structured your talk: with some Awesome Afters you want people to learn, a single focused Diamond to share, a story or two to tell. What I mean is that within the framework you develop, you let the words flow naturally around the topic or points you have identified.

Never Apologise
You are the only person in the room who knows what you planned to say. If you forget to say something, you do not need to tell your audience. They don't know and mostly do not care.

A presenter at a short workshop on getting articles published in your local paper was late arriving. She began by apologising for her car breaking down. Then continued to apologise for her slides being the wrong version and leaving her laptop in her broken down car. More time wasted apologising. As her audience, we didn't really care. We wanted her to do her very best whatever the circumstances to deliver her content and help us to get into the local papers with a story about our business. She then repeated all these tales of woe when some more people turned up midway through. It became a total distraction and moved the focus onto her, instead of onto her audience.

Even if your audience came to hear someone else talk, you don't need to apologise. That is the host or the conference organiser's job. You need to start strong, give great value and make a difference. Your opening line should not be an apology.

What You Should Script and Practice Word for Word

While most of your presentation should be delivered "off the cuff", there are two elements of your presentation that I recommend you script word-for-word. You then practise delivering them until you are so confident that you could say them with your eyes closed and heart pounding. You say them verbatim, but not with a script in front of you.

Every presentation is bookended by the two most important elements of your entire talk: your opening and closing lines. These are the things your audience is most likely to remember from everything you say. Given their importance, you need to spend plenty of time preparing them so that you know EXACTLY what you are going to say.

Let's be honest, if you get the first-line wrong, you needn't have bothered with what follows, as your audience is no longer paying attention.

Why You Need to Focus on your Opening and Closing Lines

There are two phrases that are important when it comes to opening and closing presentations – they are primacy and recency. Research has shown that our brains are most likely to remember the first things we hear (primacy) and the last things (recency). Therefore, it is vital that you place information you most want your audience to remember at the start and the end of your presentation.

Regardless of the research, it is also incredibly helpful to you, the presenter. If you get nervous when you are speaking or presenting, then one thing that can help is to have a great opening line or two. They will really help you get over those initial nerves. Most speakers are only really nervous before they speak, and then for the first few sentences. After that, they relax, realise the audience isn't going to eat them alive and the rest flows more naturally.

If you craft a really good opening line and then practise it until it's word perfect every single time, then you can relax at the start of your presentation, because you know exactly what you are going to say. You know it is strong, powerful and will grab your audience.

The end is just as powerful, yet few presenters design a killer closing line to match their opening. Too many presenters let their words and impact just fade away. They finish with "That's it" or "I have run out of time, so thank you" or just "thank you".

Even if you plan to let your audience ask questions, you certainly don't want that to be the last thing they hear. What would happen to the mood of the room if the final question undermined your Diamond or contradicted your story? Is that really the last thing you want your audience to hear before they leave?

If you are running a workshop and are using a feedback form, then you need to consider how you can plant your final sentence in the minds of your audience after they have filled in the forms. It is not that difficult to remind your audience that you have some final words to share after they have handed in their forms. Most people, while dying to rush off, will be polite enough to stick around a little while longer to hear your final words.

When your audience leaves, people are going to ask them "What did they say?" It is therefore vitally important that you have planted a powerful phrase onto the tip of their tongue and the top of their mind that your audience can tell someone else.

You want your audience to leave inspired to action, with a clear sense of what comes next. So you really need to ensure that your closing line is powerful, inspiring and gets them to take action.

A Great Opening Will Hook Your Audience
Most people in your audience will have forgotten the reason they have come to listen to you, your talk title will have been forgotten, or the invitation filed away in their email system weeks ago. Some

may have a conference schedule or a copy of your information to hand. Others will be sat, ready and waiting.

Then the room stills, silence fills the room, you can feel the anticipation on the hairs on the back of your neck, as you stand waiting to speak. Those microseconds before you speak, that is one of the powerful moments you have.

You have their undivided attention. The silence draws them in.
And then you start to speak.

You want your opening lines to make them curious, to grab their attention, to let them know that they are in the right place.

Yet so many people throw this moment away.

It's not about grabbing their attention, you already have it. It's about not throwing that attention away with something boring, predictable or banal that has them reaching for their phones and muttering under their breath.

You Can Lose their Attention in Just 3 Words
The worst possible opening is: "My name is…"
What I call an Eminem opening, after his lyrics "My name is, my name is, my name is Slim Shady".

Equally painful variations include:
"I am [name], [job title] in [division] at [company name.]" Your audience likely cares even less about your job title, the division or department you work in, or your company name

"[Company] began in 1852 when two brothers..." Your audience does not care about the illustrious history of your company either. Do not tell them about yourself UNTIL you have demonstrated that you care about them and can help them.

"I am going to talk about [topic] today" Hopefully that is obvious, but instead of telling them what you are going to tell them, say something that demonstrates what your opinion or your Diamond is.

The truth of the matter is that your audience doesn't care what your name is. Either you are a celebrity, in which case they will recognise you, or you are a nobody to them, and your name doesn't really matter. But how will they remember me? I hear you cry

Let's deal with the issue of your name. Some of you are probably quite attached to it. But ask yourself (and be honest) does your audience desperately need to know what your name is?

Even if the answer is yes, you don't necessarily need them to hear your name out loud as part of your presentation. You might have it on the handouts, or on a follow-up email, or on your title slide.

If you feel the answer is YES, then you have two options:

1. Someone else introduces you - a host, a conference organiser, a compere. If that is the case, then why would you repeat it?
2. You introduce yourself. If you absolutely feel that you HAVE to tell people your name, fine. But not until you have already hooked their attention, so that they cannot wait to listen to what else you have to say.

Your name should never the very first thing out of your mouth. Because unless your name is a hook in its own right, no-one really cares.

You want to hook your audience into listening. Dangle a fat juicy carrot in front of them, promise them something they really want or need. Your opening line might be:
"Imagine that you're handcuffed to a rocket. A fuse is lit and you have just seconds before the rocket goes off, what do you do?"

Do you think that would have an audience interested and paying full attention? You bet it would. Far more than *"I am Abe, a locksmith and I know everything there is to know about locks."*

How to Craft an Opening Line that Hooks Your Audience's Attention Instantly

Ask a Question – Or Even Better a Series of Questions

One way to get your audience involved with your first words is to ask a question that your audience really wants to know the answer to.

"Would you like to know how you can double your business while spending every Friday on the Golf Course and plenty of time with your family every weekend?"

If you were talking about networking or the power of clarity in your business marketing, you might start with a question that is both surprising and intriguing:

"Have you ever had someone rush up to you after hearing your elevator pitch and say "how much? I really need to work with you"? If not, would you like them to?"

Or something that clearly explains the opportunities that your audience most wants to take advantage of:

"How many of you have ever felt that if only more people understood what you do that you would have a queue of clients dying to work with you?"

Or something that taps into the phrases that run through their head when they are lying awake at night:

"Have you ever thought of just jacking it all in and getting a proper job, because you are fed up with being in debt and your partner constantly asking

you how you're going to pay the mortgage this month?"

You might also start with a quick poll – asking people to raise their hands for instance in response to questions such as *"Who in this audience would like…."*

Tell a Story

One way to let your audience know that they are going to get great value from listening to you would be to tell a story about someone like them. Someone who has already put into practice the skills you are going to share with them. When I talk about the importance of a networking pitch, one of my opening lines is this:

"Joanne dreaded networking. She felt that everyone glazed over when she said she was a bookkeeper and thought it was boring. Yet now she is busy, busy and knows the secret of effortlessly attracting more clients without spending lots of money on marketing."

Say Something Controversial, Shocking or Unexpected

Whatever your audience is expecting to hear, you might decide to shake them up a bit. Be careful that you do not use trite sayings that USED to be shocking but have no impact such as:

"If you are not part of the solution, you are part of the problem."

A client of mine used the following opening lines to her audience of project managers who were looking at risk in large construction projects. *"Failure is not an option. Failure is your new best friend".*

If you are talking about marketing to a group of business owners, you might start with the direct opposite of what they are expecting to hear: *"Stop Marketing Your Company. You do not need advertising, you don't need salespeople, you don't need a website or business cards. It is all a waste of your time and money."*

You might then go on to say that without a strategy, it's a total gamble. Or that instead of pursuing every single marketing opportunity they need to focus on finding the one best strategy for their best clients to find them.

Use Surprising Statistics
The use of the phrase "surprising" is important. Statistics that are over familiar have no power to hook your audience's attention. Would anyone really be surprised if your presentation's opening line were *"People are more afraid of public speaking than death. In a survey, death came third and presenting came first".* Unless of course, your talk was about the misuse of statistics from the internet, or how surveys are misinterpreted to suit the media.

However, if you were discussing personal impact, what if you said this:
"1. Not even one whole second. 1/10th of a second. That is how quickly people form their

first impressions of you. 2, 3, 4, 5, 6 , 7. Seven seconds. By now they have made up their mind about you."

Say Something Intriguing
In researching thousands of presentation titles, one that really jumped out from the list was: "Why You Never Wash a Rental Car." While it made sense, it was not clear what the talk would be about or why it might be relevant. But it got me so curious I had to Google it and find out more.

Get Your Audience to Dream Big
You might get your audience to imagine how their life or business could be better if only they already knew what you are about to tell them. So you might say:
"Imagine your alarm going off tomorrow morning. You turn it off feeling excited. You quickly bounce out of bed, full of energy and enthusiasm. You feel more than just rested, you feel on top of the world, invincible even...."

With these ideas, you can craft an opening line that will have your audience leaning in to hear more. And how are you going to finish your presentation?

A Great Close Inspires Your Audience to Action
The last thing you say needs to echo through the minds of your audience as they leave the venue. It should be on the tip of their tongue when someone asks them "how was it?" or "what did

they say?"

You want them to leave feeling confident, feeling powerful. You want them to leave eager to put the skills you have given them into practice. You want them to leave feeling that this new brighter future is just within reach. You want them to leave inspired to take action.

The Worst Possible Closing Lines
These are some uninspiring and very common closes that you should avoid at all costs because they all make your audience feel that you have run out of steam. Your audience needs more energy at the end of your speech, not less.
- The Warner Bros close: *That's all folks!*
- *Thank you for listening*
- *Any Questions?*
- *I'm sorry I seem to have run out of time.....*
- *Oh. That's the last slide*

How You Can Create a Compelling Closing Line?

Refresh Their Vision of How Their Lives Will Be Better Using Your Diamond
One of the best ways to do that is to inspire them with a clear idea of how their life is going to improve: *"If you want to have [X] then starting right now, you need to do [Y]"*

In delivering a workshop to inspire Cancer Champions to have conversations with the public about the signs and symptoms of cancer, I wanted them to leave feeling they were part of a community of people who were making a real difference. So my final two lines were these: *"Cancer Champions save lives. You are a Cancer Champion."* When I read those lines now, a third line might have made the ending even stronger: *"Every conversation you have about cancer could save someone's life."*

Here are the final lines that Bill Gates used in his talk at Harvard Commencement in 2007: *"And I hope you will come back here to Harvard in 20 years from now and reflect on what you have done with your talent and your energy. I hope you will judge yourself not on your professional accomplishments alone, but also on how well you have addressed the world's deepest inequalities... on how well you treated people a world away who have nothing in common with you but their humanity. Good luck!"*

A Story
You might decide to close by telling a powerful story of how someone's life has changed by using the Diamond in your presentation. Or you might finish a story that you started at the beginning of your presentation.

The Diamond in Your Talk
This is the one piece of information your audience really needs to know. And your closing remarks are the one of the aspects your audience remember the most. So why not reiterate the core message of your presentation? You might say something like:

"You don't need to spend any more time or money on marketing your business. What you need most of all if you want your business to grow, if you want more clients, is a simple and powerful story that demonstrates why someone would hire you. You need a Cinderella story."

With Urgency

You might decide to light a fire under your audience in such a way that they act right away, not later.

"You might have made a note to ring your client tomorrow, at 9am. You might think that is soon enough. I want you to know that you need to do it right now. Tomorrow may be too late. If you wait, you may have lost the sale, and lost it to the person in this room who rings the minute they are in the corridor. Are you really going to chance it and wait until tomorrow?"

The Bits Inbetween

Now the bits inbetween your curiosity-inspiring opening and your action-inspiring closing can be more spontaneous and unscripted. The rest of the journey needs to flow, it needs to have a rhythm that feels natural not forced. So when you are practising the content, think about the links between the various Awesome Afters and your Diamond.

Here are a few strategies that might help you to structure the flow of your presentation:

Timeline – Start to Finish

As the expert, if you want your audience to get from where they are now to somewhere else, then you might take them through the content as a chronological sequence. When you learn to drive a car, your instructor gives you a sequence to learn: mirror, signal, and manoeuvre. Other skills have similar sequences that are best learnt in order, and it makes it easy for your audience to see how the tasks link and create the end result.

For instance, if you are helping people to get a book published, the starting point is not approaching publishers. The starting point may be to decide on who is going to read it.

From Simple to Complex

When clients are very new to presenting, the most appropriate starting point is not how to animate your slides or handle a remote mouse. The starting point may be things like breathing, self-confidence, or dealing with nerves.

Whilst that is not the same as the order in this book (because delivery comes after you have designed a Presentation that Ignites your Audience), it's no good working with someone to develop a sparkling presentation if they are unable to speak when they stand in front of the room.

From Past to Present to Future

This could be considered a variation on the theme of Timeline, but it's more powerful than that. It applies to corporate strategies, product development and other timelines that span years or decades.

One of the most powerful structures is actually this: Present, Past, Future.
You start by discussing what is happening now in your organisation, industry or products. Then you may reflect on the journey to where you are now, by discussing the history of the product or organisation (where it's directly relevant, not as an indulgent flash back to your illustrious Victorian founders). Then you introduce ideas about the future that you need your audience to work towards.

Problem-Solution or Opportunity Knocks Twice
This structure works best when you want to influence an audience to change what they do in order to achieve new results.

You might begin by discussing the current situation at a high level (the impact perhaps) and then at an individual level. The individual level must not be missed out, because people will relate more to what the organisational challenge or problem means to them on a personal level than they may at an organisational level. If your audience can feel the frustration or personal pain of the problem, they will be more motivated to take the actions required to solve it.

The economy is a macro-level problem. Poor sales may be an organisational level problem.

That everyone's bonus might be at risk is a personal issue that may help trigger a change.

A merger is a high-level problem. Having individuals working alongside you who use different terms to mean the same stage in a product development will frustrate people and cause them to tear their hair out with confusion.

The solution must appear simple and realistic. The things you are asking them to do differently must be within their control and be linked to the problem as already stated. You might ask them to recommend the new product when they make a related purchase at the till to boost sales, suggesting that just 15 products a week would mean that the sales were back on target and the bonus would be paid next year.

Three Act Play

This structure is a development of the Problem-Solution format.
Act I – you talk about the current situation your audience is facing
Act II – you discuss the possible future, the promised land. Think "I have a dream."
Act III – you provide a "call to action" or a series of things your audience needs to do or think in order for that future – the promised land – to happen.

Go With Your Gut

1. You might reflect on your particular talk or topic and think that none of the above apply. That's fine. Then you can use the following method to develop a flow:
2. Write down the key points of the talk on scraps of paper or sticky notes
3. Write down any stories you think your audience really NEEDS to hear
4. Thinking of your audience and your presentation's Diamond, now move the various points around on a table. Think about the connection between adjacent ideas or points – how would you leave one and seamlessly move onto the next? If it feels unnatural, then the flow is probably out of joint. Keep going until you feel the flow works.
5. Then try it out – it doesn't need to be perfect, but you need to feel that there is a flow between the various elements and you are not stumbling over the order of the ideas.

When I was developing a short 60 second networking pitch, I wanted to introduce the idea of the tiny elephant in your hand. It was very close to the Royal Wedding and it seemed that the elephant should be the colour of the UK flag – the Union Jack. However many times I practised the pitch, the elephant was always purple. In the end, I gave up my Royal theme and stuck with what seemed to be working best for me. Sometimes you have to go with the flow, instead of fighting to jimmy something clever into your talk.

Your Delivery Makes All the Difference

The whole point of a live presentation is to have you, the presenter bring the words to life. Your energy, your intonation, your passion, your emotion will make all the difference. As I mentioned at the start of the book, there is no such thing as a boring topic. There is only a bored presenter.

If you want your audience to leave energised and inspired, then you need to be energetic and inspiring yourself. You need to be able to connect with your content. If you don't care about what you are going to say, then how do you expect your audience to care?

Your Voice – Tone, Pace, Timbre

Your pace has a big impact on your audience. At my first big presentation to a large audience of my peers and senior managers, my mouth went into top gear and afterwards my manager told me I had a "machine gun style" delivery. No wonder my talk finished in half the time!

You need to be heard. Full stop.
In large venues, that may mean a microphone. It makes your life easier if it is a clip-on microphone – although for ladies, finding somewhere to put the transmitter / battery pack can be more difficult than for men who tend to wear trousers

with pockets. What can be more of a challenge is using a handheld microphone. If you know that you will be using one, practice using one at home. The more you move the microphone around, the less stable your volume will be. If you are also using a remote mouse, you might find both your hands have something in them, which can feel quite unnatural until you get used to it.

If you are using a static microphone on a stand, then you will need to practice standing at a fixed distance from the microphone – only moving in closer to emphasise a point. Any rocking motion, either front to back or left to right, will not only be a visual distraction to your audience, but will also mean your voice fades in and out, making half your words disappear.

If you are talking excitedly, your pace is likely to speed up. When talking about sad things or problems, it is quite normal for your pace to slow down.

Silence
One of the most powerful and under-exploited aspects of your delivery is silence.
When you pause...

When you say and do nothing, your audience's attention becomes focused again. They may stop whatever they are doing and wait. Use it sparingly to draw emphasis to key points or parts of your story that need it. If you have just told them something shocking, let it sink in, or your next line will trip all over their emotional reaction.

If you go silent, then lean into your audience and in whispered tones ask "do you want to know a secret?" Your audience is almost honour bound to stop fidgeting, lean in and listen. If they don't, then that indicates you have yet to create rapport with them.

Your Body Language
How straight you stand, how upright your posture is, how you use your hands and gestures will all have an impact. Getting yourself videoed is a fantastic way to determine if you are moving unnecessarily, or if your gestures are too distracting.

A presenter who was talking all about posture and body language had the habit of constantly tilting her head slightly over to one side. That slight angle gave her a questioning or apologetic stance that undermined her powerful tips and messages.

Your Facial Expressions
One of the reasons it is important that you are well-lit when you are presenting, and not in the shadows while your slides shine brightly, is so that your audience can see your facial expressions. If you frown, you indicate something about what you are saying.

Smiling is very important to help your audience relax as you walk onto the stage, unless you have some bad news to share, when it would be creepy and inappropriate.

Your audience needs to see your expressions as it enhances your words and intonation. Look around the room when you are presenting, so everyone gets to look at you. All your expressions either complement or contradict your words.

Your Brain is Your Best Friend or Your Worst Enemy

Delivering a presentation is no more difficult than talking to your friends. The stakes may be higher, especially if it is a presentation for a new role or a promotion. You have more people listening to you. The environment and venue are unusual and more formal in many instances.

But the actual act is no different. You open your mouth and words come out. It's what happens in your brain before you talk and as you are talking that make all the difference.

You might set unreasonably high expectations for your presentation – that it will be 100% perfect. That's fine, as long as you realise that stumbling over your words is normal, and hence perfect. As is forgetting what you meant to say, which you might find happens when you are having dinner with your family as well. It's also normal that some people won't find your talk as exhilarating as others.

If you focus on doing your best, in giving your audience great value and sharing one valuable Diamond, then anything else is a bonus.

If you are hoping for a standing ovation, if you want your audience to carry you on their shoulders down the street and out into the town centre chanting your name, if you want everyone to think you are the most charismatic person they have ever met and fall slightly in love with you, then you are in the wrong place. It's no wonder you get nervous.

How to Relax Before You Open Your Mouth and Speak
Being nervous is normal.
Even seasoned presenters can feel nervous as they go onto the stage and present. After twenty years of presenting, some situations can have the butterflies in my stomach making me regret my choice of career. In other circumstances, you will barely notice them at all.

There are a number of things you can do to help yourself relax before you speak:
1. **Breathe.** If you are nervous, you will tend to breathe in short, shallow breaths. So breathing deeply, right from your diaphragm, can help you to calm down. Long, slow, deep breaths and at least three of them.
2. **"This is going to be fun!"** Nervous presenters can have all sorts of thoughts running through their heads about forgetting what they will say, about how the audience will hate them,

how they wish they had never said they would speak. A confident presenter will take positive steps to replace those thoughts with more empowering ones. My personal favourites are "this is going to be fun" and "I am going to make a difference to my audience today".

3. **Focus on Giving Value.** Nerves are all about YOU. But presenting is never about you, it's always about your audience. If you start thinking about how you are going to help your audience, then you will find your nerves dissipate. Because then it doesn't matter if you miss a bit out that you planned to say, or if you stammer a little bit, providing you get your Diamond across and some Awesome Afters.

4. **Get Happy.** Listening to your favourite music when you are getting ready is a great way to create a positive mood. Or think about someone or something that makes you smile. By deliberately creating positive experiences that you love, your nerves will disappear, as it is impossible for your brain to hold onto two conflicting thoughts at a time. So flush out your negative thoughts with positive ones.

5. **It is Only a Presentation.** When all is said and done, this is only a few minutes of your life. You might go blank (I have). You might knock over the lectern (not yet, but it's only a matter of time), you might forget to say something (all the time). But your audience will forgive you, providing you are humble and deliver real value.

6. **Your audience is nervous too.** Think about it – they have no idea if you are going to be interesting or as bland as margarine. And they are trapped in a seat with nowhere to run. They want you to be good. They want you to be passionate. They want you to be interesting. They really, really, don't want you to be nervous because that makes them squirm and feel uncomfortable.

7. **It is Just a Conversation.** Think of your presentation as a conversation. In a location where you can relax – your living room, down the pub, in the staff canteen. You wouldn't get nervous thinking about talking to your friends or colleagues. A presentation is just the same. Except that most of your audience don't get a word in edgeways. That's all.

Go out and enjoy yourself. Because your audience will mirror your emotions. If you don't enjoy presenting, they will not enjoy listening. If you are not passionate about what you believe in, guess what? Your audience won't be either.

One of my favourite quotes to help me relax is this:

"Nerves are vanity."

So where is your focus? On giving great value to your audience, or on whether or not your audience will like you. Do you want to be everyone's friend or to solve their problems?

Time For You to Know the Flow

✓ Time to craft an opening hook – you might start telling a story which you finish as your closing lines. This creates a gap in the minds of your audience, who then need to pay attention to find out how it finishes.

✓ Think about how you can inspire your audience to put into practice what they have learnt – what image or vision of the future would ensure they left feeling motivated and knowing that they can do it too?

✓ Practice your opening and closing lines until you are certain that they will have the impact you desire.

Will Your Presentation Ignite Your Audience?

If you have completed the actions at the end of every section, your presentation will have:

✓ A powerful story that highlights how your Diamond has already made a difference to an organisation or individual

✓ A clear and valuable Diamond – a singular focus that will provide incredible value to your audience, even if they remember nothing else

✓ A set of Awesome Afters to ensure that the ripple effects of your presentation continue to make a difference in the lives of those listening once they have left the room

✓ A few Remarkable Resources that keep your audience attentive and enhance your words in ways that make your presentation memorable

✓ A natural flow and rhythm of your presentation, from its opening hook to the closing lines that inspire your audience to take action

This book is not alive, or not yet. The information and advice contained in this book will only come alive when you start to act on it. When you next prepare a presentation and decide on your talk title, when you Mine for Your Diamond, when you keep your computer closed until you know what you need to say.

If you invest just an hour of your time, as the presenter you will personally benefit from:

✓ **Speed.** This process will drastically reduce the amount of time you spend preparing your presentation. Most presentations can be prepared in around 1 hour – although your resources and practice may take a little longer.

✓ **Flexibility.** You can prepare just about anywhere. You can Mine for Your Diamond on a train, on the bus, in a coffee shop, at the beach. You don't need WIFI, a laptop or even your phone. You just need paper and pen.

✓ **Confidence.** You will know exactly what you need to say, your opening and closing lines and have the confidence that your audience is going to learn exactly what they most need to learn.

✓ **Adaptability.** If your time is suddenly cut in two because someone has overrun, you can quickly glance through your notes and concentrate on your Diamond and Awesome Afters. Stories are easy to adapt to suit a new target end time.

✓ **Expert Status.** The best experts make complex things appear simple. This process is designed for your very best knowledge to shine. You will shine. Your presentation will be focussed, simple and powerful. Your audience will be delighted.

Every single step is designed to help your Presentation Ignite Your Audience. Not just inspire them, but to ignite them into action, to do something differently.

The next step is yours. Good luck and let me know if I can help.

The choice is yours, you can keep on doing what you have already done and what you have seen others do, or you can take some simple steps to add SPARK to your content, so that your Presentation Ignites Your Audience.